Other books by this author:

To order, call 1-800-765-6955.
    Visit us at www.reviewandherald.com for information on other
Review and Herald® products.

*Larry*
# LICHTENWALTER

# DAVID

# FAITH ON THE RUN

REVIEW AND HERALD® PUBLISHING ASSOCIATION
HAGERSTOWN, MD 21740

The author assumes full responsibility for the accuracy of all facts and quotations as cited in this book.

Scripture quotations credited to CEV are from the Contemporary English Version. Copyright © American Bible Society 1991, 1995. Used by permission.

Scripture quotations credited to Message are taken from *The Message.* Copyright © 1993, 1994, 1995, 1996, 2000, 2001, 2002. Used by permission of NavPress Publishing Group.

Scripture quotations marked NASB are from the *New American Standard Bible,* copyright © 1960, 1962, 1963, 1968, 1971, 1972, 1973, 1975, 1977, 1994 by The Lockman Foundation. Used by permission.

Texts credited to NIV are from the *Holy Bible, New International Version.* Copyright © 1973, 1978, 1984, International Bible Society. Used by permission of Zondervan Bible Publishers.

Texts credited to NKJV are from the New King James Version. Copyright © 1979, 1980, 1982 by Thomas Nelson, Inc. Used by permission. All rights reserved.

Scripture quotations marked NLT are taken from the *Holy Bible,* New Living Translation, copyright © 1996. Used by permission of Tyndale House Publishers, Inc., Wheaton, Illinois 60189. All rights reserved.

Bible texts credited to NRSV are from the New Revised Standard Version of the Bible, copyright © 1989 by the Division of Christian Education of the National Council of the Churches of Christ in the U.S.A. Used by permission.

Bible texts credited to Phillips are from J. B. Phillips: *The New Testament in Modern English,* Revised Edition. © J. B. Phillips 1958, 1960, 1972. Used by permission of Macmillan Publishing Co.

Bible texts credited to TEV are from the *Good News Bible*—Old Testament: Copyright © American Bible Society 1976, 1992; New Testament: Copyright © American Bible Society 1966, 1971, 1976, 1992.

This book was
Edited by Gerald Wheeler
Copyedited by Delma Miller and James Cavil
Cover designed by Luemas Design
Cover illustration by Craig Nelson/Bernstein & Andriulli, Inc.
Interior designed by Tina Ivany
Typeset: 11/14 Berkeley

PRINTED IN U.S.A.

08 07 06 05 04          5 4 3 2 1

**R&H Cataloging Service**
Lichtenwalter, Larry Lee, 1952-
    David–faith on the run.
      1. David, king of Israel.  I. Title.


             221.4092


ISBN 0-8280-1770-0

# CONTENTS

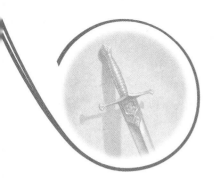

Introduction

# THE FUGITIVE

D r. Richard Kimble, a successful surgeon, had been accused, tried, convicted, and sentenced to die for a crime he did not commit—the gruesome murder of his wife. Lt. Gerard was taking Kimble to prison to be executed when the train in which they were riding suddenly derailed. When Kimble escaped, it set in motion a massive manhunt by the relentless detective. While Gerard searched for Kimble, Kimble hunted for the one-armed man he had seen murder his wife. Back and forth across the country, taking odd jobs and new identities, and constantly on the verge of being caught by the tenacious Gerard, Kimble kept looking for the real killer. It was an epic quest with the sustained suspense of high drama, close calls, and narrow escapes that lasted through four highly successful TV seasons. ABC's 1960s classic *The Fugitive* held the imagination of millions. As a boy I would beg my parents to let me stay up on Tuesday nights to watch the weekly 10:00 p.m. episode.

*The Fugitive's* concluding two episodes included a climactic chase in which Gerard during the last minute learns the truth and finds himself forced to shoot the one-armed man in order to save the doctor's life. The final episode—aired on August 29, 1967—had more viewers than any single episode in the history of TV. Seventy-two percent of those watching TV that August night tuned in to *The Fugitive*. It would be another 13 years before the television industry again achieved that kind of viewer audience (*Dynasty*'s "Who Shot JR?" episode).

David's fugitive years are a captivating saga of high drama, twists and turns, intrigue, close calls, and narrow escapes. The last 14 chapters of 1 Samuel report the epic quest that spanned nearly 11 years of David's life—King Saul dogging his steps every day—hunting, chasing, waiting for the opportunity to wipe him off the earth (1 Sam. 18:9, 29; 23:14).

It wasn't just Saul that David had to fear—the entire army of Israel was committed to his capture and death as well (1 Sam. 19:1; 23:8). Everywhere there lurked informants who would reveal David's whereabouts. Individuals who would twist the truth about his activities or label his motives. Or the self-serving who would change their loyalties and turn David in for some advantage (1 Sam. 21:7; 23:12; 25:10, 11). Israel's national manhunt became a bizarre preoccupation throwing the country into dysfunction and spiritual malaise. "God," David says at one point of reflection, "I am running to you for dear life; the chase is wild" (Ps. 7:1, Message).[1] The biblical story of that relentless chase is just as wild. It will keep you reading and wondering what's next. Will David make it—not just with his life, but with his heart? When it's all over, will David still have *a heart like His?* Will his passion for God hold out?

The biblical account of David is a tale of overwhelming passion for God.[2] Scenes from his shepherd years provide vivid imagery of his fervor and wholeheartedness when God first became the absolute center of his everything. They are filled with so much innocence, energy, vigor, and simple faith. There we find how David felt more passionately about God than about anything else in the world.[3] How his strongest instinct was to relate his life to the Lord of Israel. How in comparison, nothing else seemed to matter at all.[4] The single most characteristic thing about David was his relationship to God. The future king opened his heart to God, loved God, believed God, thought about God, imagined God, addressed God, prayed to God, sang to God, and obeyed God. David framed his whole world around God. When the Lord looked through the land in search of a new king for Israel as a replacement for Saul, only David had the kind of heart whose strongest instinct was to relate its life to God. He is the only recorded human being ever referred to by God Himself as having *a heart like His.*

David early nurtured the heart qualities and disciplines that would both awaken and sustain passion for God. When we review his shepherd years we find several facets of his passion for God that we also can value in our own relationship with God.[5] As I read these things about David's passion for God, I cannot help saying to myself, "That's what I want. Passion. David's passion. Passion for God. And I never want to lose it!"

A passion is necessary in my walk with God lest everything become mindless or spiritless.[6] I shudder at the thought that I would ever come to the place where I "go through the motions"—performing out of habit more than anything else. Or that my faith experience lacks energy because I have allocated it toward something other than God (the pursuit of a career position, a hobby or recreational effort, or some activity that appears more daring, more pleasurable, or more personally affirming). Do God and faith and my Adventist hope still grab my imagination the way they did in my younger years when I first believed? When Jesus comes, will He find spiritual passion still burning in me? My heart resists boredom or lukewarmness. I never want to be lukewarm. How about you? This is why I keep thumbing back to the story of David. I know no better model for a passionate relationship with God. This is why the Lord wants me to know David—His desire is that I too will have *a heart like his/His*. A God-saturated life filled with passion for Him!

But life's experiences can affect our spiritual passion.[7] Some will threaten it, jade it, drain it away. Our inner personal world can absorb just so much. Although we could reason that we should be ready to take it all in and respond in ease, we all too often aren't so prepared. David's 11 anxiety-filled fugitive years sorely tested him. It was one of the deepest, longest, and darkest valleys of his entire life. He had proved faithful among the sheep and competent in Saul's court. Undaunted on the battlefield with Goliath, he had distinguished himself by leading Israel's army from one impressive victory to another. And then he went from the highest pinnacle of popularity to the lowest depression of rejection and despair.[8] The emotional whiplash from such an abrupt fall would strain any spiritual passion.

David's encounters with the lion, the bear, Goliath, and the Philistine armies required courage and faith in God on a short-term basis. Although high-pressure, high-intensity challenges, they were brief and focused outward. Then David found trials of a longer lasting nature in which God often seemed far away and enemies lurked close by in every shadow. His fugitive years became a marathon of uncertainty and existential chaos in which jealousy and false accusation created genuine danger both within and without. Such things were harder for David to bear, partly because they brought with them the experience of injustice, and partly because there seemed to be no escape from their consequences—damage to his reputation, family, means of livelihood, emotional well-being, status in society, and the ability to live peacefully and safely in the place of one's choosing.

It is the nature of false accusers and the jealous that they do not easily go away and leave us in peace. The things they cause grow out of proportion, then gain the upper hand. Add a relentless threat to life, and you have an equation for real passion-destroying agony. Such circumstances can allow numbness or weariness—spiritual and emotional exhaustion—to overwhelm you. When in that weariness you give way to fear, experience the embarrassment of failure, or feel the pain of guilt because of some moral or spiritual compromise, it further erodes your spiritual passion.

The 14 chapters that Scripture invests in David's 11 fugitive years (in comparison with the 38 chapters it spends on the events of David's 40 royal years or the just two chapters for his shepherd years) suggests that this period of his life is an important one. It is as if God is saying, "Understanding David's years of hardship when he moved from faith to fear is more important than knowing his years of comparative ease and triumph. How David's passion for Me fared during his fugitive years is just as vital as how it emerged during his shepherd years and how it played out and finally triumphed in his royal years."

This volume continues a three-part journey through David's epic story in search of what it means to have passion for God. What is a passion for God really like? Can it be sustained? What might threaten it? Why is God worthy of such a thing? Do I have such a passion? Do you? If not, where do I (we) find its source? I come to David's story to find answers to such haunting questions simply because there is no better biblical model for a passionate relationship with God than his life. His colorful biography encompasses three distinct periods that highlight his passion for God from varying perspectives—his shepherd years, his fugitive years, and the years he reigned as Israel's king. The first volume, *A Heart Like His,* focuses on the initial spiritual passion of David's shepherd years when God first became the absolute center of his existence.

This volume, *Faith on the Run*, explores how the intense pressures and trials of his fugitive years threatened to destroy his passion for God. As with David, our inner personal world can cope with just so much. Although we could reason that we should be ready to respond to anything, we all too often aren't so prepared. David's fugitive years highlight some of the issues that slowly drain off zeal and threaten to leave us with loss of heart. We need to consider them in our own relationship with God.

Here we catch a glimpse of *faith on the run*—faith as it plays out in the realities of day-to-day life. Faith challenged and buffeted and perhaps retreating because some things may be too much for us. We find ourselves required to respond with hardly an instant to weigh options or motives, to determine right from wrong. As with David in this period of his life, our faith is often on the run. Sometimes it discovers itself in retreat as it struggles with almost overwhelming failure or constant and wearying pressure. But always it is on the run, whether forward or backward, because a life of passion for God is never static. It keeps moving because the circumstances and experiences of life around us don't stand still. We can never say that we have arrived, nor can we ever say that we have failed for good.

In David's fugitive years we encounter the real-life failures of a man who once carried a giant's head. As we follow David into the deepest and longest valley of his entire life we learn how he both blew it and at the same time still continued to grow. We see how fear, jealousy, pride, envy, lack of faith, a competitive spirit, anger, lying and other mental-attitude sins (both on our own part or by others) can overcome us. They can threaten and sap our passion. It is here that I find myself plummeting with David into some of the darkest areas of my inner life—into the very depths of my own sinful nature.

Many things about David inspire us toward the most noble human emotions and behavior. I see so many things in him that I wish I had, but here—in his fugitive years—I come face-to-face with some things that I'm scared I actually do have. His experience touches my most guarded and hidden emotions. As my imagination draws me into the drama of these 11 years I am stirred, shocked, amazed, and forced to think a few hard thoughts about myself. What about my own pride? Or jealousy? My ambitions or integrity? How do I handle anger and dashed hopes? And my grip on God? When the going gets rough, do I go it alone or lean on Him? I cannot journey through David's fugitive years without my world of motives and feelings and ambitions coming into focus. Here I learn, too, that we can come to the place where we doubt both God's motives and His actions.

It's hard to keep perspective when our faith is on the run. David's fugitive years give us some bearings. They tell us the kind of things to expect, some of the important issues that we all deal with. Knowing some of them as we run enables our faith to run well and our passion for God to remain. We can also learn to trust God in a new way! In the process we can become a new man or woman, wholehearted and passionate for God.

The third volume in this series, *A Passion for God,* tells of the triumphs and fiascoes of David's royal years (with all their leadership, family life, and ethical opportunities and dilemmas). It celebrates how he passionately lived large for God till the very end of life. In those years David experienced his own passionate aspiration: "I will sing to the Lord as long as I live. I will praise my God to my last breath!" (Ps. 104:33, NLT).[9] The long march of years doesn't preclude passion. Nor need our initial passion for God ever diminish. As with David, our passion for God can radiate long and deep within—until we breathe our last or Jesus comes. This is what I want. It is what I pray for as you read this volume about faith on the run and come to grips with the things that create a weariness that saps every positive quality and energy we need to be effective followers of God.

The story of David, though, is more about God than the human being. Its purpose is to reveal God to us—to show us what He is like and what He has done. Through the human being David, our Creator opens to us something about Himself. *Faith on the run*—retreating, advancing? What does that tell us about God?

When working with a wild horse, its trainers often use a snubbing post. They tie the horse to a strong post with a 30-foot rope. Each time the horse, in its struggle, gets the slightest bit nearer the post, the trainers yank the slack in. As the horse continues to buck, twist, and resist the rope, they draw the animal in bit by bit, until its nose is right down against the foot of the post.[10] David's fugitive years were God's graduate school of character-building for His future king.[11] Each episode in the unfolding story moves David close toward God's snubbing post—total dependence on Him. God gradually moved David from any naive, unwitting, or chosen self-reliance to total God-reliance. Such a course seems strange after David had whipped Goliath, doesn't it? But that's the nature of spiritual passion and the reality of faith on the run. Here, too, we find the incredible promise that at such snubbing moments God promises a way of escape (1 Cor. 10:13)!

Oswald Chambers' *My Utmost for His Highest* reading for February 14 is titled "The Discipline of Heeding." After quoting Matthew 10:27—"What I tell you in darkness, that speak ye in light: and what ye hear in the ear, that preach ye upon the housetops"—he writes: "At times God puts us through the discipline of darkness to teach us to heed Him. Song birds are taught to sing in the dark, and we are put into the shadow of God's hand until we learn to hear Him. 'What I tell you in darkness'—watch where God puts you into darkness, and when you are there keep your mouth shut. Are you in the dark just now in your circumstances, or in your life with God? Then remain quiet. If you open your mouth in the dark, you will talk in the wrong mood: darkness is the time to listen. Don't talk to other people about it; don't read books to find out the reason of the darkness, but listen and heed. If you talk to other people, you cannot hear what God is saying. When you are in the dark, listen, and God will give you a very precious message for someone else when you get into the light. . . . Now He gives you the gift of humiliation which brings the softness of heart that will always listen to God *now.*"[12]

By learning to hear in the dark we will then have something profound to say about God in the light! Spiritual passion and the dark are linked. Faith on the run will always teach us something about God—if we will but listen. Like David and the songbirds, we'll have something to sing from our darkness.

---

[1] The title of Psalm 7 associates it with a particular event (or circumstance) in the life of David during which a certain Benjaminite named Cush laid false charges against David, purporting that he had acted treacherously. Scholars are divided as to whether this false accusation by Cush took place in the presence of Saul, or that the name Cush may be a covert allusion to Saul himself (who also was a Benjaminite). The Talmud suggests that Cush the Benjaminite means Saul, thus recalling the enmity between David and Israel's first king. While Psalm 7:4 presents a number of difficulties in respect to meaning, it appears that David protests that instead of taking advantage of him "that was at peace" with him, he has done just the opposite: he has rescued the man who was at war with him without cause. This would be true of his dealings with Saul. So, far from being guilty of the offense charged on him, David, on two occasions, spared Saul's life (1 Sam. 24; 26). This

nuance appears in the CEV, *New Jerusalem,* and KJV readings of the text. It is well documented that David experienced opposition from the Benjaminites, both during Saul's lifetime and afterward, as well as from Saul himself (1 Sam. 24-26; 2 Sam. 16:5; 20:1). See Peter C. Craigie, *Psalms 1-50* (Waco, Tex.: Word Books, 1983), p. 99; F. B. Meyer, *Gems From the Psalms* (Westchester, Ill.: Good News Publishers, 1976), p. 16; *The Seventh-day Adventist Bible Commentary* (Washington, D.C.: Review and Herald Pub. Assn., 1976), vol. 3, pp. 644, 645.

[2] See my discussion in Larry L. Lichtenwalter, *David: A Heart Like His* (Hagerstown, Md.: Review and Herald Pub. Assn., 2003).

[3] Philip Yancey, *Reaching for the Invisible God* (Grand Rapids: Zondervan Publishing House, 2000), p. 190.

[4] *Ibid.,* p. 192.

[5] David's experience with God involves nine facets: 1. Passion claims it all—one's whole being. It is what the heart seeks, but it demands the whole heart—all the heart and soul and strength and mind. Everything or nothing. Only when passion claims the whole heart can we say that it has truly seized us rather than our trying to create it or fake it. 2. Passion yields it all. It not only *claims it all,* it presses the heart to *yield it all* as well. You cannot have passion if you are not willing to yield yourself fully to whatever that passion has been awakened toward. 3. Passion is imaginative. It fills the heart with art. Nothing remains status quo or colorless. Rather, it produces inspiration that leads to creativity and freshness. When passion *claims it all* and *yields it all* for some compelling cause or experience or object or being or relationship, an imaginativeness frames everything one does. 4. Passion constantly renews itself. Yesterday's passion cannot be today's inner energy. Passion quickly dissipates and must be restored regularly. By nature passion gravitates toward whatever inspires it, thirsting for more of it—thus renewing itself. Living by your passion keeps your passion stirred. 5. Passion hears what it wants to hear. It is selective, choosing who or what it listens to. It will not open itself indiscriminately to just any voice or influence that might sidetrack its vision, focus, or vitality. 6. Passion has purpose, a reason for being, an agenda—something that it is willing to spend and be spent for. Without a purpose or reason for being, passion is either impossible or empty—mere emotionalism, zeal without knowledge, real meaning, or direction. 7. Passion haunts the imagination—our worldview. Whatever vision of reality dominates our inner private world will become our passion. Once passion for something awakens, it can so dominate our perception of reality that it will both imprint with and cement our imagination on its vision. 8. Passion evokes passion. Your passion for some cause or someone can spark a similar response in another individual's life. That responding passion can be either positive or negative, stimulating or intimidating. We can turn people on or off, drawing them to us or driving them away from both us as people and whatever is important to us. 9. Passion is deeply personal, because it is experienced and expressed by a personal being— you, me, or God. It involves the meaning of our lives and the purpose of our existence. Furthermore, passion is personal because it is experienced and expressed most powerfully and most perfectly when directed toward another personal being. Intimacy makes life a passion (see Lichtenwalter, *David: A Heart Like His,* pp. 125-127).

[6] Gordon MacDonald, *Restoring Your Spiritual Passion* (Nashville: Oliver-Nelson Books, 1986), p. 8.

[7] *Ibid.,* p. 37.

[8] Charles R. Swindoll, *David: A Man of Passion and Destiny* (Dallas, Tex.: Word Publishing, 1997), p. 51.

[9] While Psalm 104 names no author, we find many indications of David's touch, and the Septuagint claims it for David (see F. B. Meyer, *Gems From the Psalms* [Westchester,

Ill.: Good News Publishers, 1976], p. 168; and Derek Kidner, *Psalms 73-150* [Inter-Varsity Press, 1975], p. 367). In Psalm 63:4 David utters similar sentiments, "I will bless you as long as I live" (NRSV).

[10] Keith Kaynor, *When God Chooses: The Life of David* (Schaumburg, Ill.: Regular Baptist Press, 1989), p. 59.

[11] *Ibid.,* p. 61.

[12] Oswald Chambers, *My Utmost for His Highest* (Westwood, N.J.: Barbour and Company, Inc., 1935), reading for February 14.

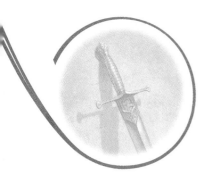

I

# THE PRICE OF POPULARITY

## I Samuel 18:5–19:17

Strangely enough, David's fugitive years began with a song! After he slew Goliath he became an instant national hero. People flocked around him to learn his name, question him, relive the enemy's defeat, and be near the youthful hero. Even Abner, Israel's military commander, heaped praise on David and brought him to King Saul for even more honors (1 Sam. 17:57). Imagine David standing before the king, Goliath's severed head in hand. What a sight that must have been. And how embarrassing and astonishing to every fainthearted person present in that field command tent—Saul and Abner included. The sudden turn of events—and the youthful hero holding the giant's head by the hair—shook everyone. Interestingly, David had often been in Saul's home. He had played the harp to soothe the emotionally troubled king. The king even wanted to keep him there full-time. Now, though, David's bravery on the battlefield so shook the king that he was not really sure who David actually was. *This can't be my musician!* "Whose son are you, young man?" he asked.

Immediately following his conversation with the king that day, David's relationship with the royal family changed forever. For one thing, Saul's oldest son, Jonathan, the crown prince, found himself irresistibly drawn to David. Scripture relates how "the soul of Jonathan was knit to the soul of David, and Jonathan loved him as himself" (1 Sam. 18:1, NASB). Jonathan loved and admired David so much that he stripped himself of his princely robe and garments and gave them, along with his sword and bow and belt, to David (verses 3, 4). A lasting and mutual friendship began that would later prove to be of supreme importance to David. This was understandable because David and Jonathan had much in common. They were both courageous and capable warriors who possessed profound faith in the Lord. Both had initiated faith-motivated attacks against militarily superior Philistines that had resulted in great victories for Israel. The surprising thing about their incredible friendship was that Jonathan was old enough to be David's father.[1]

Not only did David's relationship with Jonathan evolve that day, but so did his one with the king. David became a permanent member of the royal household. Up to this point, even though he had had access to Saul's court as court musician, David had also periodically gone home to tend his father's sheep and in the process to renew his spiritual passion after the jading experience of court life. From that day on, however, Saul kept David with him at the palace and wouldn't let him return home (verse 2). The king realized that he had found a valuable man in David and rewarded him with special assignments that soon led to a significant promotion. "Whatever Saul sent him to do, David did it so successfully that Saul gave him a high rank in the army" (verse 5, NIV). Everyone celebrated David's phenomenal success (verse 5). Even Saul's servants revered David. Here was a true test of David's popularity. Of all people, they could have become jealous, for David had not only become one of them, he overshadowed and outstripped them (verse 30).

Definitely on the rise, he enjoyed personal intimacy with the royal family and also held the heart and imagination of the common people and Saul's officers in both court and military. Popular and deeply loved, David was thus present in Saul's world in all his attractiveness, ambiguity, danger, and power—and he had also become a potentially threatening member of the king's court.

For a while it appeared that David had no enemies in Israel. He was well on his way—the king's son, the people, and Saul's officers and servants were all on his side. Everything was fine until the women began singing!

It was a national celebration. The people of Israel turned out en masse to greet the victorious army following the Philistine campaign. All along the homeward march grateful mothers, wives, and daughters met the triumphant soldiers. The women sang and danced to the accompaniment of a variety of musical instruments (verse 6). It was an ancient Israelite custom for women to compose songs with lyrics that memorialized the men's military successes (cf. Ex. 15:21; Judges 5:1-31). As happens on such a public occasion, a new celebrative song emerged saluting both Saul and David. Scripture preserves just two lines of lyrics: "Saul has slain his thousands, and David his ten thousands" (1 Sam. 18:7, NKJV). One gets the impression that the women may have vied with one another, from city to city, in demonstrations of joy of every kind. With stringed instruments, tambourines, and trumpets they came out, and exulting and moving to and fro in rhythmic dances, they cried out ever anew in responsive song, "Saul has slain his thousands, and David his ten thousands."[2] The song was an instant hit, becoming number one on the popular music chart.

Brueggemann notes that it is probable that their song, which was about "thousands" and "ten thousands," simply used two words meaning "many," and that it intended to celebrate Saul and David equally in their achievement of victory. Didn't the triumph belong to both of them? After all, they had different roles—Saul as commander, David as warrior. What reason was there to imagine tension or competition between them? Victory has no need for destructive comparison. Certainly there was enough joy for both to share equally.[3] Or was there? Sharing the limelight can be hard.

As Saul heard those words sung over and over and over on that triumphal march home, they triggered memories he wished he could forget—but couldn't. He couldn't help remembering Samuel's pronouncement that the Lord had "sought for Himself a man after His own heart" to replace him as king (1 Sam. 13:14, NKJV). Undoubtedly he felt a prophetic fulfillment in David's sudden popularity and shifting public affection. And he sensed, too, the confusing, green-eyed feelings that many get when they know in their heart that—in comparison to someone (such as David) who had shown faith, courage, passion—they have been fearful, cowardly, halfhearted, and indecisive. It gets real confusing when you are being celebrated for something you are not. When you know deep down inside that the applause over you isn't really deserved, but that the applause for the one sharing the limelight with you, or who has taken the spotlight from you, is deserving. At such moments spiritual passion drains right out of your soul.

## Popularity Has Its Price

Popularity tests both you and those around you. And when it tests those around you, it winds up examining you from another direction. The kind of success that engenders the popularity David experienced can be intoxicating. It can fuel two passion-destroying inner battles—those against ambition and pride.

Pride is the inability to handle success. We watch all too often the crashes of men and women boosted by the public to heights never thought possible before. The pain and moral compromise that so often accompanies popularity is undeniable. People hitting the top often reach bottom in their moral and spiritual life.[4] Their passion for God gets lost in the emotional rush of public affection and praise. Why? Because the applause and adulation are seductive and blinding. Generating pride in all but the most vigilant, they cause us to begin weighing every word and action in terms of how it will affect people's feelings about us. And they effectively squelch spiritual passion because the desire to impress others overcomes the passion to advance the interests of God.[5] The more we strive to live off the applause of others, the less we will hunger for the passion that motivates us to seek the approval of God. "Pride," says Oswald Chambers, "is the deification of self."[6] When we turn self into our god, passion for God Himself inevitably wanes. He no longer has all our heart, nor does He pervade our imagination. Our identity is radically shifted as we become the center of our world.

Ambition is the urge to get ahead, to establish oneself powerfully and securely. It can tempt a person to weigh every situation in terms of the possibilities of advancing into positions of fame and reward.[7] Because a close parallel exists between raw personal ambition and the spiritually passionate desire to advance the kingdom of God, ambition is a difficult spiritual enemy to pin down.[8] Do we have *holy ambition* or are we *wholly ambitious?*[9] Sometimes it's difficult at first to tell the difference between the two. It is this dual quality that perplexes us. Good, holy ambition drives the mills of excellence, helping to accomplish tasks the unambitious or passionless might deem impossible. It is the kind of energy that led David to pick up five smooth stones and head for Goliath. A striking mark of holy ambition is that it elevates God and not the ambitious striver. Passion for God always engenders holy ambition.

But raw ambition—personal aggrandizement, the quest for position and esteem, the desire to claw one's way to the top—produces an unholy product: human pride, the temptation to use people, a competitive or jealous mind-set, a lot of human "doing" rather than human "being," and following one's own agenda rather than God's.[10] Success and popularity have a way of fueling ambition. Once tasted, their quest can be intoxicating and unsatiable. As with pride, ambition can distort our identity and undermine our integrity. In the end, such self-promotion brings divine displacement.[11] We place ourselves or some coveted accomplishment ahead of God. When that happens, our passion for God Himself dissipates. It's a given: spiritual passion and ambition cannot share the same space.[12]

Popularity thus tested David's passion for God.[13] The people loved him. The troops followed him. The royal servants liked him. Everything he did was a great success. He behaved himself more wisely than all the servants of Saul. Everyone knew his name (1 Sam. 18:5, 14, 15, 30). The continual success and applause that David experienced now threatened to fuel the twin drives of pride and ambition. The inner battle that such feelings triggered was real, subtle, and seductive. Given the measure of his success and popularity, there was only one danger in David's world that could bring him down—the evil that ambushes from within. His success and popularity would demand an inner vigilance, a self-transparency and honesty, and an overriding passion for God that would both expose and crowd out feelings of pride and ambition. The spiritual attack would be relentless. David would need to shine a light regularly into his heart to discover what might lurk there. If left untouched, pride and ambition would inevitably emerge at his most vulnerable times and when he least expected.

But David knew how to live with success and the popularity it engendered without having it affect him. Scripture repeatedly tells us that he *behaved himself wisely* in all his ways (verses 5, 14, 15, 30). The Hebrew word translated "prosper" or "success" (*sakal*) most often means "to act wisely or to act with understanding." The *New American Standard Bible* reads "prospered" or "prospering" in the text (verses 5, 14, 15), but in the margin it indicates "acting wisely" or "acting very wisely." But verse 30 puts the earlier marginal reading in the text, throwing out the notion of "success" or "prospering" altogether: "David *behaved himself more wisely* than all the servants of Saul" (NASB). The two perspectives go hand in hand. Genuine *success* or *prospering* comes only when one is *acting wisely, acting with understanding*. People not only experience success and the popularity it engenders by acting wisely; they must also act with understanding as they attain that very success and popularity if they are to maintain them and keep their moral spiritual equilibrium in the process.

Such acting with understanding no doubt refers to the particulars of what one becomes successful in. For David it was the details of the assignments Saul gave him as well as the leadership skills necessary to successfully command Israel's soldiers (verses 5, 30). But behaving wisely also touches one's inner spiritual world of motives and values and responses. In the case of David that meant coming to grips with pride and ambition. Keeping a close monitor on his motives, values, and responses, he had to make sure they were honorable, worthy, and righteous. The key to his continued success and popularity was always his ingrained character. As his popularity increased, David wisely drew upon such internal resources as patience, modesty, caution, maturity, forethought, and faith.[14]

The profound statement that David acted wisely "for the Lord was with him" (verse 14) places his *understanding* in context. As Psalm 111 asserts: "The fear of the Lord is the beginning of wisdom; all those who practice it have a good understanding [a good success]" (verse 10, NRSV). If you want to have a good understanding of things, people, and God, you will get it best by being right with Him. The standpoint from which we view things is of the utmost importance to our right understanding of them. Here again, the margin gives another reading for the Hebrew word *sakal*—"a good success." Act up to all that you know and you will come to know even more (John 17:7). Do God's will and perform the inner spiritual disciplines that keep you in His will. Be careful about your motives and values and responses. Keep a handle on pride and ambition. And the Lord will be with you, prospering you,[15] just as He was with David.

Our most difficult times are not when things are going hard. Hard times create dependent people. Survival keeps you humble. But when success comes, everything's swinging in your direction, and you have a passion to accomplish some heady goal—that's the time to watch out. That is when you are the most vulnerable, because you feel the least accountable and will lose spiritual and moral concentration. At that point you need the kind of pride and ambition-rejecting perspective that only God's presence in your life can bring.

## Handling Personal Jealousy

Once as the devil crossed the Libyan desert he came upon a spot where a number of small fiends were tormenting a holy hermit. The saintly man easily shook off their evil suggestions. After watching their failed attacks, the devil stepped forward to give them a lesson. "What you do is too crude," he said. "Permit me for one moment." With that he whispered to the holy man, "Your brother has just been made bishop of Alexandria." A scowl of malignant jealousy at once clouded the previously serene face of the hermit. "That," said the devil to his imps, "is the sort of thing I recommend."[16]

Tasting popularity not only tests you; it does the same thing to those around you. There are always those who become jealous because you are more well liked or more successful than they are. Jealousy is the fear of losing something you already have or the fear of losing something that you think should be yours by right. When I envy, I want what you have. And when I'm jealous, I'm afraid I'll lose what I already have to you. Or I'm afraid that I'll lose to you what I think's coming to me.[17] The severest form of jealousy normally emerges when the popularity of one person supersedes that of another.[18] That's what happened with Saul. He had been Israel's national hero (1 Sam. 10:24), a great warrior (1 Sam. 14:47, 48). David unintentionally challenged Saul's popularity when he slew Goliath. As the women lauded the younger man's outstanding bravery in song, David's popularity replaced Saul's. Suddenly he had to share the limelight, and it was hard. Imagine yourself in a similar situation. It's as if you were being replaced— just like that! All of a sudden you are a nobody, or so it seems. And so Saul hears the women's song through the filter of his jealousy, because it celebrated David either as his equal or as his superior (1 Sam. 18:8).

At least three passion-destroying emotions accompany jealousy, and

Saul experienced them all. First, he became "very angry" (verse 8, NKJV). The Hebrew word for the kind of anger Saul experienced is informative: *charah* means "to burn, be kindled with fire, glow with anger, heat oneself with vexation." Unlike some of its synonyms, *charah* points to the fire or heat of anger after it has just ignited. It captures the moment a person explodes with anger, the instant before any sense of control takes over or they even have a rational thought. Rarely do we accomplish anything profitable at the moment we become angry. Actions or words immediately following the flare-up of anger are almost always regrettable. And such anger blinds our passion for God.

The second emotion Saul faced was suspicion. Losing his objectivity, he began to perceive David as a threat and a competitor (verse 9). He interpreted everything about the younger man through the prism of his deep and debilitating suspicion. "To me," he murmured angrily to himself, "they have ascribed but thousands, and to that one tens of thousands! Now what more can he have but the kingdom?" (see verse 8). In his insecurity and suspicion, Saul concluded that David already had all that the king could give him—except the kingdom. Now he imagined that the purpose of David's presence in his court was eventually to seize the throne. While the women's jingle did not intend to be derogatory to Saul in the process of celebrating David's outstanding bravery, in the light of Samuel's rejection of him the words seemed to point to his replacement. That suspicion forever poisoned his relationship with David. His self-talk lost control. "I got a giant-killer on my hands who's gonna become a king-killer!" Paranoia dominated his mind from that day on. From that moment Saul "kept a jealous eye" on David (verse 9, NIV). The Hebrew suggests that the king twisted or distorted his eye toward David. Saul's chosen perceptions of David warped both the younger man's motives and his actions. He would observe David carefully for one purpose—making the new hero's life miserable.[19] It is a given. Whenever jealousy fuels our imagination, suspicion takes over. When that happens, some pretty troubling, even dangerous, things can happen.[20] Jealous people can become downright evil!

Saul's third emotion was fear. "Saul was afraid of David, because the Lord was with David but had left Saul" (verse 12, NIV). The king knew deep down why everything was going wrong for him and right for David. He had alienated himself from God. When he realized that he, himself, didn't have that kind of spiritual passion—that kind of moral power, that sense of the holy presence of God deep within—it was more than he could handle.

Saul was angry, then suspicious, finally fearful. Irrational behavior follows such reactions. Soon he began looking for opportunities to kill David. The first murder attempt took place while the younger man was playing music for the king. For some time Saul had been subject to black moods and demonic visitations. David and his music had been a healing presence at such times. One day, instead of being healed, Saul responded in hate. The king hurled his spear at the court musician, muttering, "I will pin David to the wall!" (verse 11, NKJV). Seeing it coming, David ducked. The spear drove into the wall, inches from David's head. Not once, but twice, Saul hurled a spear at him (verse 11).

David's willingness to remain in the room long enough for Saul to retrieve the spear after the failed first attempt and then take a second shot at him portrays the incredible depth of his loyalty to the king and his commitment to helping Saul overcome his torments.[21] Probably David simply assumed that the king's behavior resulted from his depression and didn't take it personally. He would simply be more careful, but not fearful. Interestingly, the spear incident did incite fear—not in David, but in Saul (verse 12). The very people who are out to get us are often the ones who are most afraid of us.[22]

The initial hot, irrational, and murderous outbursts quickly escalated into cold-blooded, carefully calculated plots either to erode David's popularity or to make sure he was dead. First Saul sent David out into the field to do battle (verse 13). Failure to perform his duties successfully even once on the battlefield would reduce or erase David's prestige and popularity and perhaps even end his life.[23] The chances of David getting killed increased in proportion to the amount of time he spent on the battlefield.

Next Saul promised to give his daughter Merab in marriage to David on the condition that he prove himself in combat, exposing him to such continuous danger that the Philistines would eventually kill him (verse 17). If David had been interested in social climbing, he most certainly would have jumped at the chance, but he hesitated. "Who am I, and what is my family in Israel that I should be the king's son-in-law?" the younger man exclaimed. "My father's family is nothing!" (verse 18, NLT). Later when David showed up after the fierce Philistine encounters alive and ready for the wedding, Saul hastily married Merab off to another (verse 19). I believe that it was a conscious attempt to provoke David to some impetuous act by withdrawing his daughter from the promised marriage. Being jerked around—with changing assignments and unkept promises—can thoroughly test your spiritual passion.

When Saul learned that his daughter Michal was in love with David, he used that knowledge against him. "I will give her to him, that she may become a snare to him, and that the hand of the Philistines may be against him" (verse 21, NKJV). We know little about the daughter, but Saul considered her marriage to David a way to destroy him.

Michal would be a snare to David in two ways: first, she could motivate him to place his life at extreme risk in the ongoing conflict with the Philistines. Saul promised David that he could marry her if he would present him with 100 Philistine foreskins within a certain time period (verse 25). Surely out of 100 chances, David would get killed! The shepherd/musician/soldier didn't have the requisite dowry or social standing to marry the king's daughter on his own. He was from a poor family, while Saul's was that of royalty. So David saw Saul's offer as an honorable means of overcoming all social proprieties and paying the price for his bride. In fact, he thought it was a great idea and cheerfully went off, killed double his assigned quota, and presented the king with the obscene dowry, a sackful of 200 Philistine foreskins. This time the marriage took place: Michal became David's wife (verses 22-27).

The second way Saul knew Michal could snare David was spiritually. The term translated as "snare" is theologically significant. The Pentateuch uses it three times to describe the dangers of idols and idol worshipers (Ex. 23:33; 34:12; Deut. 7:16). Evidently Michal had idolatrous inclinations (cf: 1 Sam. 19:13). Her father was spiritually astute enough to recognize that, in marriage, such tendencies could easily lead David astray, in which case his future son-in-law would become the Lord's enemy and come to a disastrous end.[24] Either way, Saul thought, he would eventually win. His scheme is an amazing and disgusting example of what jealousy can do in our hearts. Can you imagine the evil in the heart of a man who would use his own daughter as a pawn in a personal vendetta? Saul had high hopes that Michal would be the death of David, but the young man had something greater than high hopes. He had passion for God, and because of that, the Lord was with him.

Michal's love for and marriage with David only aggravated Saul's hatred and fear (1 Sam. 18:29). David is now his son-in-law, with visible entitlement to royal power. At the same time, his exploits on the battlefield keep increasing (verse 30; 19:8). The crown prince thinks the world of David, standing up for him again and again as Saul demands that someone put his rival to death (1 Sam. 19:1). Saul is becoming a remarkably isolated and increasingly hopeless individual. Clearly recognizing that momentum has slipped from his hand, he is helpless to turn the flow of power and popularity back in his own favor.

The king's final attempt on David's life before he fled the royal court for a fugitive life in the wilderness involved assassins. Saul ordered hired killers to stake out David's house and kill him first thing in the morning. But Michal discovered the plot and helped her husband escape that night through a window. She put a dummy in his bed with a head of goat hair on it. When morning arrived, the assassins waited and waited for David to come out, but when he didn't they went in to get him. Michal told them that her husband was sick and couldn't see them. Not wanting to murder a defenseless sick man, they reported back to Saul that David was ill in bed and couldn't come out to get murdered. Exploding into rage, Saul ordered them to bring David to him, bed and all, and he himself would kill him. But when the would-be assassins arrived back at David's house, all they found in the bed was the dummy with the goat-hair wig (verses 11, 17).

Jealousy is a normal emotion. Any man would have felt threatened under the circumstances Saul faced. But God wants us to learn to understand our feelings and handle them constructively and maturely. He would have helped the king deal with his jealousy and the passion-draining emotions it engendered had Saul responded in the right way. But the monarch refused to deal with the root problem of his inner spiritual world. Pride and hardness of heart had drained his passion for God. He had never truly shown remorse for his earlier disobedience or really humbled himself before God. Saul was never ready to yield to what he knew to be divine workings. As a result, the king did not turn to God for help in dealing with his feelings. Never once did he open his inner private world for divine correction or healing. As far as we know, he never asked God to change his heart attitude.

Nor did Saul seek assistance from others. Why didn't he ask his own son, Jonathan, to help him? Jonathan's self-sacrifice and solemn allegiance to David stood in stark contrast to his father's attitude. The personal attachment and public commitment the crown prince showed David must have made Saul wonder about his own reaction, especially when Jonathan spoke well of David to him (verse 4). Such moments of personal appeal on the part of his son would have been the opportune moment for Saul to pull Jonathan aside and open his heart for help. But pride kept him from doing what was right. Because he did not seek aid from others, Saul became isolated in his jealousy and insecurity.

I wonder what would have happened had Saul been honest with David. What would have happened if he had told David exactly how he felt and then sought his personal help? No doubt he would have found assurance that the younger man was not his enemy. That he wasn't out to upstage the king. In the personal relationship that would have grown out of such intimate sharing, Saul would have had an entirely different perspective to help moderate his feelings. Opening our heart personally to the very people who threaten us will actually remove their power. When we take time to establish intimacy and transparency, we rise above the spirit of competition to where we can delight in and affirm the success and effectiveness of others. It frees us inside and allows spiritual passion to flourish.[25]

## Handling Jealousy in Others

Popularity tests you in a different kind of way when someone becomes jealous and unleashes their irrational actions against you. It is always disorienting to be attacked when we're doing something good. While we don't exactly welcome punishment for our wrong actions or failures, we don't usually feel disconcerted by it when it does happen. There's a moral logic to just deserts. We assume that we will get called on the carpet for doing wrong, for not doing a good job, or for doing something stupid, but we don't expect it for doing right, for being successful, or for behaving wisely.[26] Instead, we instinctively echo David's protest to Jonathan: "What have I done? . . . What is my crime? How have I offended your father that he is so determined to kill me?" (1 Sam. 20:1, NLT). The existential angst generated by such attacks can be incredibly exhausting and undoing. The dizzying experience of self-examination such moments engender quickly consumes our spiritual passion. It confuses us when people constantly wonder about our motives or responses. The accusation, suspicion, and irrational actions against us invade our private world and soon dominate our imagination. The effects on us—emotionally, spiritually, morally—can be debilitating.

All of us have experienced it at some point, especially if we are a leader enjoying success and the popularity that goes with it. Even if we receive 10 words of support for every one word of criticism, which voice will ring loudest? The critic's, of course. Criticism generally carries more weight with people than praise. And so with jealous suspicion, which often fuels the critical spirit. Many leaders have resigned their positions despite widespread popularity because they grew weary of a handful of unrelenting critics. Jealousy-fueled backbiting and slander can quench the spirit of even the most stouthearted person. When others routinely question our motives, or when we find our actions misjudged, the joy drains out of our heart. Success no longer satisfies. We question whether what we are doing is worth all the pain.

How did David handle Saul's jealousy? What did he do? Did he seek God's wisdom in this situation? Did he wonder about his own motives, his own responses? Was it possible that he was unwittingly using Saul's weakness to enhance his own image? Did he find himself tempted to take advantage of the situation? Often, when we threaten someone with our own skills and abilities or successes, it can give us a certain degree of emotional satisfaction. Especially when we are outperforming our superior, and everyone around us knows it. Such feelings swirl in our hearts without our even thinking. What do we do with them?

And what did David do? He turned in three directions to be sure the unfair attacks were without merit and to come to grips with any inappropriate feelings that might have been creeping into his heart. First, David looked deep within in honest self-examination. Second, he sought advice from a trusted friend to mirror back his actions and help test and understand his motives and response. "What have I done?" he protested to Jonathan. "What is my crime? How have I offended your father that he is so determined to kill me?" And, finally, David turned to God. Ultimately God's approval meant more to him than the people's, or even Saul's. When we know we have obeyed God, we can set aside our desire to defend ourselves.[27] We then find security in God's affirmation and promises. "'No weapon that is formed against you shall prosper; and every tongue that accuses you in judgment you will condemn. This is the heritage of the servants of the Lord, and their vindication is from Me,' declares the Lord" (Isa. 54:17, NASB).

Right motives, actions, and responses will prove themselves over time. We can let God demonstrate the purity of our motives and the wisdom of our actions. That's what David sought—God's vindication—because in his heart he knew he was innocent. "[Yahweh]! God! I am running to you for dear life; the chase is wild. If they catch me, I'm finished: . . . [Yahweh], if I've done what they say . . . if my hands are really that dirty, let them get me. . . . Stand up, [Yahweh]; pit your holy fury against my furious enemies. Wake up, God. My accusers have packed the courtroom; it's judgment time. Take your place at the bench, reach for the gavel, throw out the false charges against me. I'm ready, confident in your verdict: 'Innocent'" (Ps. 7:1-8, Message).

In the end, though, David didn't do much better than most of us do when facing the jealousy of others. He evidently could handle success better than he could hostile jealousy. Pride and ambition within his own heart were easier to deal with than feelings of jealousy directed toward him. Applause and adulation more than suspicion and accusation. In the course of time Saul's jealousy began to wear on him. It lingered and grew worse, even though David continued to be humble, meek, and unassuming. While he did not lose his temper or lower his personal code of ethics to compensate for the treatment he received, the pressure was unrelenting like a dripping faucet. In the process David became emotionally and spiritually exhausted and filled with confusion, doubt, and tremendous anxiety. He could have approached this *giant* with the same faith and confidence with which he had faced Goliath—but he didn't. A different kind of enemy, it would put his *faith on the run*. That's what David's fugitive years are all about—faith on the run. Faith needing to be played out in the realities of day-to-day life. Faith challenged and buffeted and perhaps retreating because some things may be too much for us.

### I Know What That's All About

Few of us can identify with what David faced the day he challenged Goliath. But all of us can identify with another *giant*—the powerful emotions stirred by success and the popularity it engenders, both in ourselves and others. None of us escape the inner battles with pride, ambition, jealousy, or with handling the jealousy of others. We've either met them in our own lives or we've encountered them in others. Emerging at the most unsuspecting times, they threaten to nullify our attempts to develop passion for God. Almost impossible to define or predict or control, they demand an inner vigilance, a self-transparency and honesty, and an overriding passion for God. We have to deal with them repeatedly and forcefully. God wants us to learn to understand our feelings and handle them constructively and maturely through His power.

And so I am forced to ask some hard questions. Do I think competitively? Am I *wholly ambitious* or is it *holy ambition* that energizes my soul? It's a fine line that I'm not always sure about. And what about pride? Can I feel good about something I have done—a satisfying sense of accomplishment or of God at work in my life—and not be proud? How do I chart those waters? Do I worry about the success of others? Do I delight in another person's success, or do I feel insecure, afraid that someone else's achievement in some way threatens my own? How do I handle personal jealousy and the passion-draining emotions it triggers in me (anger, suspicion, fear)? How do I handle jealousy in others? What do I do when I am criticized, second-guessed, or have my motives questioned?

The answers to such questions demand self-transparency and honesty. Even then I do not have the capacity to know or understand my own heart (Jer. 17:9; Prov. 14:12; 16:25; 20:24). Through earnest prayer I must ask God to search me and reveal the real interior workings of my soul. Passion when faith is on the run demands an open heart. "Examine me, O Lord, and try me; test my mind and my heart," David writes when falsely accused (Ps. 26:2, NASB). "Search me, O God, and know my heart; test me and know my thoughts. Point out anything in me that offends you, and lead me along the path of everlasting life" (Ps. 139:23, 24, NLT).

If we would be God's son or daughter at any cost, when our faith is on the run we must unveil our inner being—purposefully, consciously, right down to where unspoken thoughts dwell and unstated motives secretly lurk. We must invite God's searchlight to bathe us and expose which thoughts or tendencies lead us away from fellowship with Him. "Show them to me so I can understand them and their effect on my walk with You" should be our prayer. Authentic passion can remain only in open, transparent hearts. If we refuse to allow God to get close enough to really know what we're like (even though He already does), we'll never stay close enough to Him to keep faith when it is on the run.

[1] See Larry L. Lichtenwalter, *David: A Heart Like His,* pp. 120, 121, note 19; Keith Kaynor, *When God Chooses: The Life of David,* pp. 52-55.

[2] F. W. Krummacher, *David, King of Israel* (Grand Rapids: Kregel Publications, 1994), pp. 55, 56.

[3] Walter Brueggemann, *First and Second Samuel* (Louisville: John Knox Press, 1990), p. 136.

[4] Steven Berglas, *The Success Syndrome: Hitting Bottom When You Reach the Top* (New York: Plenum Press, 1986).

[5] G. MacDonald, *Restoring Your Spiritual Passion,* p. 114.

[6] Oswald Chambers, *My Utmost for His Highest* (reading for June 12).

[7] MacDonald, pp. 108, 109.

[8] *Ibid.,* p. 109.

[9] James D. Berkley, "Holy Ambition or Wholly Ambitious?" *Leadership* (Summer 1990): 28-35.

[10] *Ibid.,* pp. 29, 32-34.

[11] *Ibid.,* p. 33.

[12] MacDonald, p. 112.

[13] Theodore H. Epp, *A Man After the Heart of God* (Lincoln, Nebr.: Back to the Bible Publication), p. 37.

[14] Kaynor, p. 67.

[15] According to the Pentateuch, those who kept the words of the Sinai covenant would "prosper in everything" they did (Deut. 29:9, NLT). Passages with *sakal's* dual perspective of acting with understanding/experiencing success include: "I will instruct you and teach you in the way which you should go; I will counsel you with My eye upon you" (Ps. 32:8, NASB); "Keep the charge of the Lord your God, to walk in His ways, to keep His statutes, His commandments, His ordinances, and His testimonies, according to what is written in the Law of Moses, that you may succeed in all that you do and wherever you turn" (1 Kings 2:3, NASB); "God has looked down from heaven upon the sons of men to see if there is anyone who understands, who seeks after God" (Ps. 53:2, NASB).

[16] Hesketh Pearson, *Oscar Wilde: His Life and Wit* (New York: Harper and Brothers, 1946), pp. 127, 128.

[17] Betsy Cohen, *The Snow White Syndrome* (New York: Macmillan Pub. Co., 1986), p. 23.

[18] Gene A. Getz, *David: Seeking God Faithfully* (Nashville: Broadman and Holman Publishers, 1995), p. 64.

[19] Robert D. Bergen, *The New American Commentary: 1, 2 Samuel* (Nashville: Broadman and Holman Publishers, 1996), vol. 7, p. 201.

[20] C. R. Swindoll, *David: A Man of Passion and Destiny,* p. 57.

[21] Bergen, p. 201.

[22] Swindoll, p. 61.

[23] Bergen, p. 203.

[24] *Ibid.*, p. 204.

[25] Getz, pp. 66-68.

[26] Eugene Peterson, *Leap Over a Wall* (New York: Harper Collins, 1997), p. 49.

[27] Henry and Richard Blackaby, *Spiritual Leadership: Moving People On to God's Agenda* (Nashville: Broadman and Holman Publishers, 2001), p. 248.

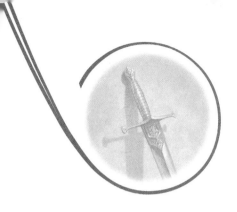

2

# UNDER THE SPELL OF GOODNESS

## I Samuel 19:1-10

Serbia's notorious paramilitary leader Arkan (whose real name was Zeljko Raznatovic) was finishing dinner at the Rotisserie French restaurant inside Belgrade's Hotel Intercontinental when an unknown number of gunmen sprayed the place with Heckler & Koch submachine guns. Arkan caught a slug in the eye—among three head wounds—and was DOA at the city's emergency hospital. The list of people who wanted Arkan dead was long. Speculation swirled as to whether he was killed because of underworld business interests, rivalry with police, or a bid to bargain with the United Nations war crimes tribunal. The war crimes tribunal had indicted him in 1997 for crimes against humanity, including atrocities in Croatia in 1991 and in the 1992-1995 Bosnian war. Many considered him responsible for the death of hundreds of Croats and Muslims allegedly killed by his paramilitary unit, known as the Tigers, that had terrorized civilians during the breakup of Yugoslavia. His men had also been implicated in the killing of more than 200 unarmed Croats abducted from the Vukovar hospital after the fall of the town in 1991.

Arkan was among the most feared leaders in the former Yugoslavia. He was also a liability. He knew too much and had taken part in many things that could implicate the then Yugoslav president Slobodan Milosevic. Someone high up in the powerful Serb political establishment obviously wanted him quiet for good.

Somehow the hardened warlord saw the handwriting on the wall, and, like any person with a price on his head, fear prompted him to shift into "survival mode." He began to worry and watch his back. *If Slobo wants to whack me,* he thought, *my only safety is to turn informant.* So two months before his assassination rumors began to circulate that Arkan was considering defecting to the West and that he was negotiating a deal with the International War Crimes Tribunal at The Hague to testify against Milosevic in return for immunity from prosecution. Arkan had also begun taking other precautions, changing homes every few nights in the posh Belgrade neighborhood he shared with other Serb luminaries and traveling with bodyguards in an armored jeep. He knew something was up. But his time ran out.[1]

David knew the kind of unnerving, godforsaken fear that bolts through someone's heart when they realize that they're marked individuals with prices on their heads. That the big people they've been faithfully serving no longer like them or need them or want them around anymore, and as a result have given them the "thumbs-down." Notice the words "David fled, and escaped," because you will read them again and again during the unfolding moments of David's fugitive years—four times in rapid succession (1 Sam. 19:10, 12, 18; cf. 20:1). Flight and escape became the pattern, a means of survival, with fear being David's driving emotion or passion.

David's fear was understandable—even predictable. Saul's attempts on his life were becoming more frequent. They shifted from a private behind-the-scenes scheme to a reckless public strategy as Saul explicitly orders his son Jonathan and all his servants to kill David (1 Sam. 19:1). Although the crown prince spoke openly with his father about David's innocence—saying many good things about his friend, reminding the king that David had not wronged him in any way but had actually benefited him greatly—Saul again tried to pin David to the wall with a javelin while David played his soothing music (verses 4-10). This time David didn't wait around for Saul to take a second shot. He fled to his home. But David's house was no protection. It became a death trap surrounded by assassins. Saul had ordered them to watch carefully David's movements in order to put him to death in the morning (verse 11). Michal, however, was aware of her father's plan and, like her brother, warned David of his danger. She urged him to flee before morning. "If you don't run for your life tonight," she cried, "tomorrow you'll be killed" (verse 11, NIV).

With her help, David slipped out a window to some unguarded spot below and scurried off to safety. Psalm 59 reveals his troubled thoughts as he literally ran for his life on that hair-raising night:[2]

"Deliver me from my enemies, O God;
protect me from those who rise up against me.
Deliver me from evildoers
and save me from bloodthirsty men.
See how they lie in wait for me!
Fierce men conspire against me
for no offense or sin of mine, O Lord.
I have done no wrong, yet they are ready to attack me.
Arise to help me; look on my plight!
O Lord God Almighty, the God of Israel,
rouse yourself. . . .
O my Strength, I watch for you;
you, O God, are my fortress, my loving God.
God will go before me
and will let me gloat over those who slander me. . . .
I will sing of your strength,
in the morning I will sing of your love;
for you are my fortress,
my refuge in times of trouble.
O my Strength, I sing praise to you;
you, O God, are my fortress, my loving God."
—Ps. 59:1-17, NIV

David's nighttime escape from an upper window of his house gives this psalm its urgency, its sense of outrage ("I have done no wrong, yet they are ready to attack me"), its scorn of the doglike nocturnal prowlers who would trap him, its desperate plea to God for help, its repeated assurances that a loving God will protect and vindicate, and its fear! Can you imagine that kind of inner struggle? The prayer to God when you realize your own home has become a death trap? Crying out to Him while you slip out a window, hoping not to be seen by those hired to kill you?

Reaching for God in the darkness while you flee for your life?

Claiming your innocence, you beg Him to look at what's going on. To rise up and do something soon! Desperately you seek to assure yourself that God cares and will protect and strengthen you. That when morning comes, rather than being dead, you will be full of life, praising Him for being your protecting fortress. In such moments one's spiritual passion may be easy to voice but hard to hold on to.

It's hard to imagine that the same David whose courage and faith led him to kill a lion and a bear and then Goliath with just a sling was now literally fleeing for his life. Previously we have seen David running toward his enemies—now he runs from them.[3] But there's a difference between the generalized fear resulting from some threatening circumstance we may find ourselves in (being under attack, terminal disease, sudden catastrophe, etc.) and the reality that we are being singled out as a target, and the support system we've been a part of has suddenly disappeared.

Most people appear to be more susceptible to fear, even panic, when they are alone, think they are alone, or have actually been abandoned.[4] Not only was David's life in danger; he was losing all his support. Everything human he might have leaned on was collapsing—his position in the king's court and in the army, his wife, his best friend, his standing among the people. In the process, things began changing in his heart. All was not well. His emotional stability began to erode. The once calm, confident warrior was feeling the squeeze. Little by little the fear of what one powerful man could do to him began to replace his faith. The reality that "there is hardly a step between me and death" (1 Sam. 20:3, NASB) now haunted him. Death dogged his steps. Ever live like that? A hair's breath away from death (or some catastrophe or failure)?

Fear can be such a powerful emotion, an overwhelming passion. The expectation of evil or the awareness of danger—and the inner anxiety it generates—can quickly change from apprehension to fear, to dread, to fright, to absolute terror. An icy hand grips you. Something squirms in your stomach and whispers in your ear. Your vision swims, your muscles tighten, and adrenaline surges through your body. Heart pounding, you run! You flee as hard as you can without knowing where you are going. My mind still fills with the images of terrified people hurtling for dear life as the World Trade Center towers collapsed behind them on September

11, 2001. As debris rained down from the sky those men and women ricocheted off of every object that stood in their way. They had but one emotion—fear. And they had one passion only—survival. The stare in their eyes and the look on their ash-covered faces told it all.

You cannot control yourself if you let fear take over your life. Fear makes you panic. It can change your personality and alter your being. By affecting the way you live your life, it steals your passion for God.

Fear is nothing more than an emotion or feeling that exists in our mind. We can't touch or hold it. And we can't show it of itself to another person. Instead, we fear certain things because of what we think might happen (or has happened). At times it is good to be fearful, but it becomes dangerous if you let fear rule your life. Most of the time what we fear is something we have never even experienced (or likely will never experience). Our mind has a hard time determining whether what is taking place is real (or will be real) or just imagined. As Mark Twain once quipped, "I have been through some terrible things in my life, some of which actually happened." One motto creates the acronym:

> False
> Evidence that
> Appears
> Real

Even when what we fear is real, fear still exists only in the mind. And we still cannot let it dominate our imagination or rule our lives. Because whether real or imagined, fear can alter our being and the way we live. And worst of all, it can rob us of our spiritual passion.

The things David feared were real—powerful and jealous people, unfolding events that left him increasingly isolated, physical threats against his life. But how would his mind perceive them? When we succumb to a view of people or events that causes them to appear to be far more powerful than the God of our faith, it leaves us emotionally, spiritually, and physically debilitated. Spiritual passion can quickly evaporate when we allow ourselves to assume that such dangers hold the real power to change and control history or to affect our lives. As David ran that night, he was struggling to keep God in the equation. Thus the prayer recorded in Psalm 59. Fear was threatening to dominate his imagination, to become his consuming passion. It's not something that David wanted, but as I've already noted, in such moments one's spiritual passion may be easy to voice, but hard to hold on to.

### What Have I Done?

Have you heard of the "wicked flea"? I have a playful friend who delights in puns, one-liners, and witty sayings. The kind of banter that catches you off guard, brings a smile, and quite often evokes an unexpected new insight into life or God's Word. He is an Old Testament scholar who has spent years mulling over the kind of technical syntactical details in Scripture that would bore most of us to death. Quite often his witticisms revolve around some idea he has toyed with in a biblical passage.

So he asked me once, "Have you heard of the 'wicked flea'?"

"What?" I answered cautiously, knowing I was likely going to get outwitted again.

"The wicked flea! It's in the Bible, you know," he answered with a wry smile, his wide eyes watching me from underneath bushy eyebrows.

My mind whirled like a CD-ROM for a few moments, trying to remember where in the world the Bible might refer to a "wicked flea."

He didn't wait long. "The *wicked flee* when no one is pursuing, but the righteous are bold as a lion" (Prov. 28:1, NASB). "Gotcha!"

According to Proverbs, a guilty conscience can cause people to run from real or imagined danger, but a good conscience makes one unafraid. Isaiah tells us that "the wicked are like the tossing sea, which cannot rest, whose waves cast up mire and mud. 'There is no peace,' says my God, 'for the wicked'" (Isa. 57:20, 21, NIV). Fugitives often struggle with conscience and haunting images because of what they may have done. Spooked by anything that might catch up with them and reveal them for what they really are, they even run away when no one is chasing them.

When David later fled from Naioth in Ramah, he came to Jonathan, saying, "What have I done? What is my iniquity? And what is my sin before your father, that he is seeking my life?" (1 Sam. 20:1, NASB). Here we catch another glimpse into David's troubled and frightened psyche. As his heart pounded from anxiety, his questions reflected his confusion, doubt, and anxiety. Under tremendous psychological pressure, he was beginning to lose his spiritual and emotional bearings. In the midst of it all he struggled with his conscience and the haunting images of what he might have done, or should have done, but didn't. By asking the question "What have I done?" David was essentially telling Jonathan that he must have done something wrong to get on Saul's most wanted list. But he couldn't pinpoint anything that he had consciously committed. If he could only nail it down, he could make it right and things would be fine again.

"What have I done?" Four times we hear David raising this probing though rhetorical question. He asked it when his oldest brother, Eliab, criticized him for expressing interest in the reward for killing Goliath (1 Sam. 17:29). Here he brings it up when he meets with Jonathan, wanting to understand why his father was out to get him (1 Sam. 20:1). One night David asked it of Saul directly after sneaking into Saul's sleeping camp and stealing his jug of water and spear (1 Sam. 26:18). Then there is the Philistine king, Achish of Gath, who requested that David not accompany the Philistine army when it went to fight against Saul (1 Sam. 29:8). "What have I done?" David queried.

Each time David raised his rhetorical question, the possible answers became problematic.[5] The fact was that he had done a lot to raise jealousy, suspicion, and persecution. His *actions* pointed steadily toward the throne, but his *intentions* were something else.

Interestingly, when David asked Saul directly, "What have I done? Or what evil is in my hand?" he referred to himself as a *flea*, "for the king of Israel has come out to search for a single flea" (1 Sam. 26:20, NASB). David, however, was no "wicked flea"—excuse the pun! The biblical narrative takes care to assert his complete innocence. Jonathan himself "spoke well of David to Saul his father and said to him, 'Do not let the king sin against his servant David, since he has not sinned against you, and since his deeds have been very beneficial to you. For he took his life in his hand and struck the Philistine, and the Lord brought about a great deliverance for all Israel; you saw it and rejoiced. Why then will you sin against innocent blood by putting David to death without a cause?'" (1 Sam. 19:4, 5, NASB). Later Israel's king himself acknowledged David's righteousness and claimed responsibility for the breakdown of their relationship: "You are more righteous than I; for you have dealt well with me, while I have dealt wickedly with you" (1 Sam. 24:17, NASB). "I have sinned. . . .

Behold, I have played the fool and have committed a serious error" (1 Sam. 26:21, NASB).

So why did David run? Shouldn't his sense of integrity have made him unafraid? Despite his innocence, David was still racked with existential self-talk. Conscience pricks whenever our lives are in turmoil, whether we are innocent or blameworthy. "What have I done?" is a question we instinctively ask when we are being treated unfairly or the circumstances of life seem to pile up against us. When coupled with fear (whether real or imagined), such existential musings of conscience further blur our perceptions of reality. Fear has a way of causing the conscience to sting deeper, and a troubled conscience has a way of making such fear paralyzing. Also what we fear now seems to be destined and inevitable. Our grip on God becomes tenuous. As Shakespeare notes: "Conscience doth make cowards of us all."

Only a clear conscience before God can enable us to endure and maintain both our faith and self-worth when fear threatens to overwhelm us. Unfortunately, David wasn't always able to hold on to such a vision of both himself and God. Nor am I—or you!

## Under the Spell of Goodness

After Michal helped David escape through an unguarded window, David ran several miles through the darkness for protection to the prophet Samuel at Naioth in Ramah. At Naioth Samuel presided over a school of prophets. We can imagine something on the order of a monastery of prophets immersing themselves in a daily round of prayer and prophesying (1 Sam. 19:18-20).[6] David must have believed that Saul would not order his troops to invade such a sacred place. By coming to Naioth, he essentially claimed sanctuary.[7]

Here David told Samuel all that had happened and how the king was determined to kill him. David went to Samuel because God had used the prophet to anoint him as Israel's next king. Probably David had questions for the old prophet. "Are you sure God told you to anoint me? If so, what should I do now? What does God have to say about all this? Is there a word from the Lord?" Samuel would understand both David's dilemma and his fear. At one point he too had known the possibility of death at the

41

hands of Saul (1 Sam. 16:2). Also Samuel could offer spiritual encourage-ment, since he was the prophet who had received the revelation of David's selection as Israel's next king. Receiving David, he no doubt confirmed the younger man's divinely appointed calling.

Aided by his intelligence network, it didn't take Saul long to locate his fugitive son-in-law (1 Sam. 19:19). Sanctuary or not, he immediately sent a posse to bring David back to the palace. Now here is where the story gets interesting. Some details in it elude our understanding, but the thrust of the account is clear enough. When Saul's officers arrived they found themselves caught up in prophetic ecstasies and overwhelmed by God's Spirit. In the process they forgot their order to arrest David (verse 20). Instead, they spent the day singing and praying. When Saul heard what happened, instead of feeling God's rebuke, he sent more men to capture David. The same thing happened to the second band of officers (verse 21). In his unabated hostil-ity and determination, Saul dispatched a third group of men—only to hear that the Spirit of God came upon them as well and stopped them from grab-bing David (verse 21). The story builds in dramatic power by the thrice-repeated statement about messengers seized by the Spirit and who then prophesy.[8] While we cannot explain the phenomenon fully (Ellen White tells us that angels constrained them), it is clear that God supernaturally thwarted them from carrying out Saul's orders. And the point? The Lord was willing and able to protect David from Saul.

By now Saul is disgusted and decides to take matters into his own hands. He too goes to Naioth. Picture him fully armed and furious about the soldiers never returning. But along the way an angel of God meets Saul and subdues him as well. The Spirit of God begins a convicting work in his mind that shatters his plans. The closer he approaches Naioth, the greater the pressure from the Holy Spirit to face his wickedness. The nearer to David he gets, the more overwhelmed and reverent he becomes. As truth bores into his mind, he faces himself honestly and falls down near the as-tonished worshipers. The Spirit of God literally holds Saul in His power.

The king had started out with murder on his mind, but he and his evil intent were no better able to withstand God's Spirit than his soldiers had been. Soon he was completely under the influence of God's Spirit, giving witness to the divine presence, praying, singing, prophesying (verses 22, 23). So much so that people asked, "Is Saul now a prophet?" (verse 24,

CEV). No, Saul was not a prophet, but like a prophet he was under the control of God. The Spirit gripped him so powerfully that Saul stripped off his outer garments that symbolized his rank. He lay, as it were, naked before Samuel and his pupils all that day and through the night under the influence of the divine Spirit (verse 24). Walter Brueggemann observes that "the pitifully embarrassing scene is that of this once great man, still tall but no longer great, exhausted by demanding religious exercise (cf. v. 24), clearly not in control, shamed, now rendered powerless in a posture of submissiveness." [9] Before the compelling, inscrutable, inexplicable power of the Holy Spirit, Saul was helpless. [10] As Peterson notes, Saul "had fallen under the spell of goodness and was rendered temporarily incapable of evil." [11]

It's an incredible story. God overruled human wrath and manifested His power to restrain evil. At the same time He walled in His servant by a guard of angels. [12] Surely God has the power to make even a demon-dominated man act like a righteous person in order to protect one of His chosen servants. [13] Can you imagine a God with such power and awesome sovereignty over human lives? In going to Naioth in Ramah, David had placed himself in a situation in which only God could help him. [14] Saul would never have changed his mind on his own. Nor could Samuel have talked the king out of his wrath. Only God could make a difference. He had to subdue the vengeance-bound king. And He did!

### Don't Miss His Message

Through this bizarre experience God communicated two vital messages. First, God was reaching out to Saul. When the Spirit of God came upon him and his men, the Lord was certainly reminding the monarch of a very special event earlier in his life when Samuel had anointed him king. It was a moment when the Spirit came upon him so mightily that he prophesied among the prophets (1 Sam. 10:10). Now it had happened again. As one writer asks: "How could Saul miss the message of this divine intervention? He was not just fighting David—he was fighting God! God was saying, loud and clear, that He was still able to change Saul's heart and life permanently—if only Saul would let Him." [15] Would the experience last? Would Saul want the work of the Spirit on his heart and life to continue? What would he choose? The Spirit's convicting influence on his mind shattered his plans. Would that be all right? The experience of the Spirit's compelling power and control caused Saul to face his wickedness. Would he humble himself in repentance and desire a change of heart?

As truth bore into his mind, Saul faced himself honestly and fell down near the worshipers. Would he stay in that posture of worship and self-honesty?[16] No, it didn't last. Saul chose to let the experience fade. And how often that is also true of you and me. Convicted of some deficit in our life, we see God's hand at work to literally restrain us from some path of evil that we're dead set on. But we don't let either that recognition or that unmistakable sovereign providence of God make any lasting difference. As we gravitate back to our old way, spiritual passion short-circuits once more.

The second message of Naioth was for David. God could and would protect and deliver him from Saul's hand. The Lord had clearly demonstrated this fact, showing that without His permission Saul and his men could not touch David. He assured the future king that He would protect him just as He had when David confronted Goliath. Such visual and dramatic affirmation could restore his spiritual passion. It could pull the plug on his fear and self-doubt. In going to Naioth, God revealed to David that he had placed himself in a situation in which only God could help him.[17] Sadly, David missed this message—just as Saul missed the one God had sent to him.[18] David's fear was too real—more real, in fact, than God seemed. That fear overshadowed God's protecting power and overwhelmed David's spiritual passion.

So he ignored the sign of God's protection and took matters into his own hands. While Saul remained constrained by the Spirit, he once again ran for his life. As he did, things continued to go from bad to worse. That's the way of fear. Fear will always overrun passion for God. If we let it dominate our imagination, God will slip out of our focus. When we choose a view of people or events that causes them to appear to be far more powerful than the God of our faith, we'll always run. And that's not hard to do.

David's problem was that he not only lost perspective on the past; he was doing the same toward the present. He not only forgot what God had done in the past (with the lion, the bear, and the giant Goliath); seemingly he even ignored what had just transpired in Naioth. Faith was on the run—but not toward God.

When fear ravages our imagination, it's hard to keep our mind on the divine. In such moments spiritual passion may be easy to voice, but hard to hold on to. We need to preserve our perspective by remembering what God has done for us in the past, to remind ourselves that "we have nothing to fear for the future, except as we shall forget the way the Lord has led us."[19] To preserve our faith we must become aware of what God is doing in the present—even the little things that seem so peripheral. Listen to His gracious promises: "Do not be afraid or discouraged, for the Lord is the one who goes before you. He will be with you; he will neither fail you nor forsake you" (Deut. 31:8, NLT). "Do not fear, for I am with you; do not anxiously look about you, for I am your God. I will strengthen you, surely I will help you, surely I will uphold you with My righteous right hand" (Isa. 41:10, NASB). "For I am the Lord your God, who upholds your right hand, who says to you, 'Do not fear, I will help you'" (verse 13, NASB).

And we must let Scripture shape our self-talk: "The Lord is my light and my salvation—whom shall I fear? The Lord is the stronghold of my life—of whom shall I be afraid? When evil men advance against me to devour my flesh, when my enemies and my foes attack me, they will stumble and fall. Though an army besiege me, my heart will not fear; though war break out against me, even then will I be confident" (Ps. 27:1-3, NIV). "The Lord is for me; so I will not be afraid. What can mere mortals do to me?" (Ps. 118:6, NLT). What we say to ourselves about God is vital when faith is on the run.

Also we must remember too that a good conscience makes one unafraid (Prov. 28:1). There is no need to run. Nothing steels spiritual passion more than an inner innocence that clings to a holy God who has not only demonstrated His power in the past and present, but promises to be with us as we step into an uncertain future.

---

[1] "Cold-blooded Justice," *Newsweek*, Jan. 24, 2000, p. 60; "Serb Warlord's Killing Sparks Many Questions," Reuters Ltd. 11 (Jan. 17, 2000): 12 "Arkan Killing Stirs Speculation," United Press International 10 (Jan. 17, 2000): 11.

[2] The title for Psalm 59 refers to this specific experience in David's life when Saul sent men to watch his house in order to kill him.

[3] Larry L. Lichtenwalter, *David: A Heart Like His*, pp. 108, 109.

[4] S. J. Rachman, *Fear and Courage* (New York: W. H. Freeman and Co., 1990), pp. 59-61.

[5] Marti J. Steussy, *David: Biblical Portraits of Power* (Columbia: University of South Carolina Press, 1999), p. 72.

[6] Eugene Peterson, *Leap Over a Wall*, p. 56. The word "Naioth" (1 Sam. 19:18) literally means "dwellings/habitations" and may refer to a religious compound within Ramah, per-

haps even the one mentioned in 9:22 (Robert D. Bergen, *1, 2 Samuel,* pp. 209, 210).

[7]Ellen G. White, *Patriarchs and Prophets* (Mountain View, Calif.: Pacific Press Pub. Assn., 1890), p. 653.

[8]Walter Brueggemann, *First and Second Samuel, Interpretation, A Bible Commentary for Teaching and Preaching* (Louisville: John Knox Press, 1990), p. 144.

[9]*Ibid.,* p. 145.

[10]*Ibid.*

[11]Peterson, p. 56.

[12]White, p. 653.

[13]Keith Kaynor, *When God Chooses: The Life of David,* p. 70.

[14]*Ibid.,* p. 69.

[15]Gene A. Getz, *David: Seeking God Faithfully,* p. 90. See White, pp. 653, 654.

[16]Kaynor, p. 70.

[17]*Ibid.,* p. 69.

[18]Getz, p. 90.

[19]White, *Life Sketches* (Mountain View, Calif.: Pacific Press Pub. Assn., 1915), p. 196; *Testimonies to Ministers* (Mountain View, Calif.: Pacific Press Pub. Assn., 1923), p. 31).

3

# HOW TO LIE TO YOUR PASTOR

## I Samuel 20:1–21:9

Fourth of July festivities at the Lichtenwalter home sometimes include Chinese firecrackers; rockets that shoot up into the sky, then burst into colorful streamers; handheld sparklers that spurt red-hot light off the glowing tips of metal rods; and those unnerving gizmos that swirl around frantically either in the air or on the ground shooting out different shades of fire and smoke—you're never sure that they won't come your way. Each of these fiery spectacles has something in common. They make you wide-eyed with their dazzling display of dancing, shooting, kaleidoscopic light. Then they fizzle. Their excitement lasts only for a few brief seconds. Once they have done their thing, they vanish, leaving you in darkness and wondering what's next.

When David witnessed Saul fall under the convicting and restraining power of the Spirit of God in Naioth at Ramah, something told him it wouldn't continue. Here Saul lay before Samuel and his pupils, stripped of his outer garments that represented his rank as king, all day long and through the night. Songs and prayers and prophecies flowed out of his mouth in an act of worship and praise like a sparkler glowing fiery and beautiful in the mighty hand of God. What an awesome moment that must have been! People flocked to witness this strange scene, and they reported their ruler's experience far and wide. "Is Saul also among the prophets?" they mused (1 Sam. 19:24).

The change that overcame Saul caused him to assure David that he was now at peace with him and that he had nothing to worry about anymore. But the fugitive had little confidence in the king's renewed spiritual passion or in his repentance.[1] He had seen Saul like this before—up, then down—and knew it would not last. The intensity of the Spirit's convicting and restraining influence would eventually subside. At some point Saul's heart would go on its own again. God would not permanently take away Saul's will or his freedom of choice. His renewed spiritual passion, deep-felt conviction, and divine restraint would be only for the moment. Saul would soon again find himself brooding in darkness.

When the Spirit came upon Saul, He rendered him temporarily incapable of evil. Also, He filled his heart with a holiness that transformed him into a humble and repentant worshiper. In the process, God was reaching out to Saul, communicating an unmistakable and urgent invitation. The Lord was saying, loud and clear, that He was still able to change Saul's heart and life permanently—not just for a day—if only the king would let Him.[2] "I can do it," God implied, "no matter your past disobedience or the darkness that swirls inside your heart. Whether you struggle with murderous jealousy, anger, or fear, or you feel abandoned by Me, I can give you a new heart! I can do it, Saul. Things are not hopeless! Here is proof. Look at what I can do." The urgent invitation attending such display of God's power would be just as unmistakable—"Let Me do it! Let Me change your heart and life permanently. Humble your heart right now, fully, completely. Let Me be God in your life. I will make this experience last forever, Saul—if you choose. Choose Me, Saul. I am only a prayer away."

Regrettably, when Saul left the spiritual atmosphere of Naioth, his heart once again said no to God. The revival of spiritual and moral conviction, the passion of worship, the humbleness before God—none of it lasted. Not because God was not willing to make it go on or because spiritual passion is unsteady or difficult to maintain. It did not continue simply because Saul chose another passion over that for God—jealous self-will. How often that is true. Convicted of some deficit in our life, we see God's unmistakable hand at work to restrain us from some path of evil we're dead set on. We experience a moment of renewed spiritual passion when He is very close, and our hearts burn within us at the hearing of His

Word, some spiritual song, or uttered prayer. God's unmistakable voice beckons our heart. The message is obvious, the invitation plain. The Lord wants to do a new thing in us not for the moment only but forever. He seeks to be the passion of our lives. And He can make it happen—if we would only yield, fully, unreservedly. But tragically, we don't let either that burning conviction or the attending display of divine restraining/re-newing providence make any lasting difference. The choice is ultimately ours. Often, like Saul, we choose another passion.

When I ponder these moments in Saul's life, I am reminded of both God's power and His invitation. It reminds me, too, of human will and freedom of choice. God has the power to transform the most darkened soul. He can make even a demon-dominated person act like a righteous individual. The Lord has the power to change the heart, affecting one's thoughts and words and actions. God can do it. Let there be no doubt about it. And He can accomplish it in you no matter how great your dis-obedience in the past or how much you might feel abandoned by God or how far away from Him you feel. He can give you a new heart! Things are not hopeless! Be encouraged! God is able! Hear the promise of God: "I will give you a new heart with new and right desires, and I will put a new spirit in you. I will take out your stony heart of sin and give you a new, obedi-ent heart. And I will put my Spirit in you so you will obey my laws and do whatever I command. . . . You will be my people, and I will be your God. I will cleanse you of your filthy behavior" (Eze. 36:26-29, NLT).

But while God has such incredible transforming power, He will not do so against our will. He will not override our freedom of choice. Passion for God, even though it is His free empowering gift, must always be will-ingly chosen.

While David had misgivings about Saul's change of heart, Jonathan thought his father had been converted for good. After such a remarkable exhibition of divine power in Saul's life, he could not believe that his father would still harm David.[3] So when David came to him crying, "Why is your father trying to kill me? What have I done wrong? What sin have I committed? Why is he doing this, Jonathan?" Saul's son replied, "Never! . . . You are not going to die! Look, my father doesn't do anything, great or small, without confiding in me. Why would he hide this from me? It's not so!" (1 Sam. 20:2, NIV). But David was not convinced. With intense earnestness he declared to Jonathan, "truly as the Lord lives and as your soul lives, there is hardly a step between me and death" (verse 3, NASB).

"So, what do you want me to do?" Jonathan finally asks (verse 4).

Thus unfolds the well-known story of the secret signal involving arrows that the two of them worked out together so Jonathan could warn David if his life truly was hanging by a thin thread.

The story told in 1 Samuel 20 is a highly dramatic one. It is filled with vivid scenes of anger and hurtful words, deep anguish and tears, and ultimately the painful parting of closest friends. By now Saul's intent to murder David has congealed into a hard, fixed purpose. Even Jonathan is at risk. The sparkler has burned out. Dark passions of jealousy and rage purposely close the door to God's Spirit and take away any remaining hope of reconciliation in David's mind. Rather than attempting to retell it here, I suggest you set this book aside for a few moments and read the account directly from the Scriptures (1 Sam. 20:1-42). As you do, let your heart connect with the emotional turmoil that David, Jonathan, and Saul experience both together and individually. By this time David's heart was deeply wounded. The emotional and psychological turmoil he had been experiencing had been unrelenting. Now, during the uneasy moments recorded in this chapter, those emotional injuries become abysmal, further depleting David's spiritual passion.[4]

The kinds of things David experienced were spiritually and emotionally exhausting. They left him devastated and disillusioned. No one has unlimited energy or passion. It can and will eventually run out. David reached the point at which he was simply drained. Wearied to the point that he lost his perspective, he felt a terrible sense of loneliness and of being stripped of everything by his enemy. All outside supports were fast fading away, and his hopes and dreams were painfully caving in.

It is difficult to grow or restore passion for God when living under such conditions. They create a weariness that saps every positive quality and energy we need to be effective followers of God. Only when we are sensitive to what's taking place both around us and within us—anticipating their passion-threatening power—can we know the emotional, spiritual, and moral issues with which we have to deal. When we can recognize and describe the passion-threatening conditions that we experience, we are then more likely to know how we should respond. While

David could graphically voice such conditions—even intuit how he should thus respond with God (as illustrated in his psalms)—his fugitive years reveal that he, like every one of us, had a difficult time keeping perspective, maintaining his spiritual energy, and sustaining his passion for God. Passion for God is difficult to hold on to when you are drained, devastated, disillusioned, and disheartened. Let's allow David's experience with these things to help us spot the times when they are most likely to occur and then guide us as to how we should respond when they do.

### Situation Ethics

Following the message of the arrows, David was now fully and unquestionably on the run—a fugitive. He fled without having a chance to pack his bags or think of a plan. Not knowing fully where he was going, he bolted for his very life. Fear was now David's driving emotion, escape his single passion. In his confusion he forgot Naioth, Ramah, where he had recently witnessed firsthand the power of God to protect him when he sought shelter at the school of the prophets. Would God not have done it again? All he needed was to put himself wholly in the sanctuary of that sacred place. Surely he would be safe there with God. But instead David ran to Nob, apparently to seek the advice of Ahimelech, the high priest (1 Sam. 21:1).

Nob, a community of priests, was a little village between Jerusalem and Gibeah. Years earlier Israel had taken the tabernacle to it after the devastating battle at Shiloh. It was here that Ahimelech ministered and the heart of Israel's worship found its center. Like many of us in times of crisis, David may have desired to draw closest to those who seemed nearest to God or to the place where God had promised His presence. Not a bad idea!

David arrived at the sanctuary at Nob breathless and weak from hunger. His unexpected appearance left Ahimelech bewildered and literally shaken. Upon seeing David, the high priest came out trembling to meet him (verse 1). The expression on David's face and the look in his eyes must have showed anxiety, anguish, and panic.[5] He was obviously alone and in a hurry. High-profile leaders such as David did not usually travel by themselves or look so bewildered. *Why is he in such a hurry and with no escort? What's going on? Is something wrong?* the high priest wondered to himself and then out loud. Surely by now knowledge of Saul's unstable emotional condition had spread throughout the whole land. His fickle jealousy and snowballing persecution of David was clearly common knowledge among Israel's leaders. Ahimelech hesitated to get involved. Such politically sensitive matters could put one's own life on the line.

It is understandable, then, why the high priest was nervous with David, but I find it interesting that David was obviously uncomfortable with Ahimelech as well. Here were two men uncertain of each other, not sure what to do.

*Is David in trouble with Saul? Is it safe for me to get involved? Should I help him?*

*What does the high priest know? Whose side is Ahimelech on? Can I trust him?*

Tell me, have you ever lied to your pastor? You know, he or she meets you either unexpectedly or perhaps planned and asks you about something—yourself, your family, your marriage, a friend, your habits, something that took place in a meeting, some conversation, something they have observed about you or were told by others—and you don't come clean? You dance around the issue or leave important information out. Or just plain lie. Maybe you see the pastor coming and quickly hide stuff or do not answer the bell when it rings. Your pastor notices all the cars in the driveway, and can't understand why no one answers the door.

Have you ever lied to your pastor?

Most of us are very private about the things going on in our lives. We are not always comfortable telling spiritual leaders the real issues we struggle with. Perhaps we may be embarrassed about the difficulties or problems we are facing. Maybe we are nervous about being found out on some controversial or sticky moral/spiritual matter we are caught up in or want to remain hidden. Conscience and fear often keep us from the very things and the very people who could help us the most. Sometimes we really want to share what's going on in our inner private world. We know that if we don't, we'll go under or burst. So we make that difficult call and set an appointment. But at the last minute our tongues get tied and we chicken out. We find ourselves playing it safe with peripheral issues or minor questions. Afterward we leave not having been honest or really helped. The spiritual counselor we came to see is still in the dark about what we actually wanted.

"Why are you alone?" Ahimelech asked. "Why is no one with you?"

"The king has sent me on a private matter," David said. "He told me not to tell anyone why I am here. I have told my men where to meet me later. Now, what is there to eat? Give me five loaves of bread or anything else you have."

"We don't have any regular bread," the priest replied. "But there is the holy bread, which I guess you can have if your young men have not slept with any women recently."

"Don't worry," David replied. "I never allow my men to be with women when they are on a campaign. And since they stay clean even on ordinary trips, how much more on this one!"

So, since there was no other food available, the priest gave him the holy bread—the bread of the presence placed before the Lord in the tabernacle. It had just been replaced that day with fresh bread.

Then David asked Ahimelech, "Do you have a spear or sword? The king's business was so urgent that I didn't even have time to grab a weapon!"

"I only have the sword of Goliath the Philistine, whom you killed in the valley of Elah," the priest answered. "It is wrapped in a cloth behind the ephod. Take that if you want it, for there is nothing else here."

"There is nothing like it!" David said. "Give it to me!" (1 Sam. 21:1-9, NLT).

Without doubt David was hungry. And he did need a sword. But there was more going on than he dared admit. Much deeper things. And Ahimelech had the right to know the truth! David had come to see the servant of God. But in that awkward moment of meeting his spiritual counselor he did what many people do. Fearful of discovery, in his extremity he made up a story and reassured Ahimelech by lying to him. He gave the false impression that he was alone because he was on a secret mission for Saul. Then he stretched his yarn by adding that the men accompanying him on his assignment had hidden somewhere nearby so as to preserve secrecy (verse 2). How many times I have reacted similarly through the years!

One of David's first downward steps in his slide from faith to fear was lying. Actually, he was already caught in a maze of lies, surrounded by lying people. Everyone around him was distorting truth in one way or another. Saul had lied to him (1 Sam. 18:21). The king's servants had lied to him (verse 22). His wife, Michal, had lied for him so that he could escape, and then turned around and lied against him in order to protect her own life and reputation (1 Sam. 19:14, 17). It was easy, then, for David to adopt the same manner of dealing with life's difficult situations. Even the scheme he and Jonathan worked out with the arrows involved deception. It involved a little twisting of the facts in order to gain some information about Saul's real feelings about David. David had not shown up to eat at the king's table during an important festivity. When Saul asked Jonathan, "Why hasn't the son of Jesse been here for dinner either yesterday or today?" his son replied, "David earnestly asked me if he could go to Bethlehem. He wanted to take part in a family sacrifice. His brother demanded that he be there, so I told him he could go. That's why he isn't here" (1 Sam. 20:26-29, NLT). But David had not attended the yearly family feast in Bethlehem, as Jonathan led his father to believe. The younger man was hiding in the field, scared out of his wits. Saul knew Jonathan was lying and exploded with anger, hurling a javelin at his own son.

Once you start down the path of falsehood it's easier to lie a second time—and a third and so on. You can get to the place where you can even lie to your pastor.

In his dishonesty with the high priest David applied a "situation ethic." He assumed that his situation was of such a serious nature, such a dire need, that the greatest good (protecting his life, getting food, information, and a weapon) could be accomplished by resorting to a compromising standard of conduct—lying.[6] The ends justified the means! People do strange things when their faith is on the run.

Is it all right to lie in certain circumstances? For example, when you are a fugitive? How else could you escape? Doesn't fleeing demand deception? Isn't one's life more valuable than a person's word? Who has the right to know the truth, anyway? Certainly not your enemy. Not the one out to kill you. But what about your pastor?

## Playing God . . .

A man went to his rabbi with a question. "Rabbi," he said, "I understand almost all of the law. I understand the commandment not to kill. I understand the commandment not to steal. What I don't know is why there is a commandment against slandering my neighbor."

The rabbi looked at the man and said, "I will give you an answer, but first I have a task for you. I would like you to gather a sack of feathers and place a single feather on the doorstep of each house in the village. When you have finished, return for your answer."

The man did as told and soon returned to the rabbi to announce that he had completed the task. "Now, Rabbi, give me the answer to my question. Why is it wrong to slander my neighbor?"

"Ah," the rabbi said. "One more thing. I want you to go back and collect all the feathers before I give you the answer."

"But Rabbi," the man protested, "the feathers will be impossible to collect. The wind will have blown them away."

"So it is with the lies we tell about our neighbors," the rabbi said. "They can never be retrieved. They are like feathers in the wind."

It's a given that we cannot retrieve the wrong done by the lies we tell, either in slander, duplicity, deceit, or fraud. We cannot halt the consequences of a lying tongue once it has unleashed some falsehood. Every untruth wounds and warps relationships. Every falsehood erodes spiritual passion by undermining our God-consciousness. Somehow in the process of telling lies, God gets left out of the picture.

While he may have fooled Ahimelech, David's lie became a feather in the wind. Doeg the Edomite, one of Saul's chief shepherds, was also in Nob that day. He too saw David. Word soon got back to Saul. "When I was at Nob," Doeg informed the king, "I saw David talking to Ahimelech the priest. Ahimelech consulted the Lord to find out what David should do. Then he gave David food and the sword of Goliath the Philistine" (1 Sam. 22:9, 10, NLT). The results of David's lie in this case were tragic. Saul immediately called for Ahimelech and his whole family of priests. Irate and irrational, the king accused Ahimelech of protecting David and of helping him escape. No explanation was acceptable. Saul ordered Ahimelech's death as well as the execution of all the priests present that day—85 in all. Then Saul ordered an attack on the city of Nob, and his men killed "both men and women, children and infants; also oxen, donkeys, and sheep" (verse 19, NASB). Only one priest survived.

All because David lied. Later he painfully regretted ever going to Nob. As he told Abiathar, the massacre's lone survivor, "I knew on that day, when Doeg the Edomite was there, that he would surely tell Saul. I have brought about the death of every person in your father's household" (verse 22, NASB). At the time, David didn't see the potential harm of telling his lie. It seemed to meet the immediate need very well. But it had disastrous effects. His apparently harmless tale indirectly caused the death of 85 priests and their families. A whole village suffered from that one lie. That's a heavy load for anyone's conscience. The remorse from that kind of responsibility can steal the passion right out of your heart. God's presence and God's forgiveness can feel so far away. Who can have spiritual passion in moments like that? David would have done anything to take that lie back. But it had gone forth, and having done so, it was no longer under his control. It would go on producing its diabolical fruits both in the lives of others and in his own. David could repent and find assurance of forgiveness, yet it would not miraculously restore the people of Nob to life.

Ellen White contends that "had the facts been plainly stated, Ahimelech would have known what course to pursue to preserve his life."[7] In other words, had David told Ahimelech the truth, the high priest and his family would not have perished. Keith Kaynor presses a similar point as he observes that "when David lied to Ahimelech, robbing him of responsible, intelligent choice, he was *playing God* for Ahimelech and the others who would ultimately be involved. He may have wanted to spare Ahimelech any involvement in the misery of his situation; he may have thought he was doing the priest a favor, allowing him to be able to tell the king that he was honestly unaware that David was fleeing from him. However, David may have deliberately kept the priest uninformed, afraid that if he knew the situation fully he would refuse to help. In either case, David made a decision that was really Ahimelech's burden."[8] David was a faithful and respected leader in Saul's government, the kind of individual that the king would be likely to select for a secret mission. Ahimelech had little reason to doubt what David told him, though he was fearful. Little did he know that he would soon die because of his involvement with the musician/military leader. Had David clearly stated the facts, the high priest would have known what course to pursue to preserve his life.

That's an interesting perspective, don't you think? That when David lied, he was usurping the role of God. He was creating (distorting) reality with his words and in the process robbing Ahimelech and his family of responsible, intelligent choice—something a truthful God will never do. It was a paradox. On the one hand, David was playing Deity with his lies. On the other, he was totally unlike God, who is both true and trustworthy. Tragically, when we are playing God for others, the God we are depicting is no longer our passion. As happened with David, when we find ourselves under pressure we may claim that our situation justifies lying. We, too, may play God for others by giving partial, distorted, or exaggerated information or by withholding data that people need in order to reach an informed choice. When people make decisions based on full knowledge, they are ready to bear the consequences.[9] If we would be like God before them, we will be truthful in every way.

Commenting on this tragic moment in David's life, Ellen White further asserts that "God requires that truthfulness shall mark His people, even in the greatest peril."[10] In other words, absolutely no experience in life justifies falsehood—even the greatest peril that we can imagine. Such absolute integrity demands incredible faith and complete trust in God. It requires a passion for Him that overrides every other, including the desire to save one's own skin. In Scripture, life is not the ultimate value (Rev. 12:11; 2:10)—honoring God is. Truthfulness honors God.

God's end-time people display impeccable and unquestionable integrity, even amid great peril of life and fortune. No lie lurks in the mouths of those who follow the Lamb (Rev. 14:5). They imitate Christ's truthfulness—for He is faithful and true (Rev. 19:11; 3:14). The people of God reflect Him in both word and action. The important contrast in the Apocalypse between the forces of evil and the Lamb's followers is that between deceit and truth—what comes out of one's mouth. Only truthful people will be able to enter the Holy City in the earth made new (Rev. 21:27; 22:14, 15). The truthfulness expressed here is not merely doctrinal, nor its focus solely on accurately reflecting God and His truth to a deluded world. The truthfulness that the book of Revelation envisions touches every sphere of our lives. Being truthful is not what we do as much as who we are. Only truthful people can hope to speak truthfully. If we are to be honest with others, we must be honest with ourselves. Being dishonest with others ends in falsifying ourselves—a consequent loss of spiritual passion.

Trust is the foundation of all relationships. Community requires openness and honesty. No genuine community can exist between false selves. Integrity sets me free to live with my brother or sister. I can look into his or her eyes. And integrity allows him or her to live with me. Even more fundamentally, integrity means being whole for oneself too—and for God! By being free within and clean, able to live without guilt or shame, such integrity allows me to look both into the mirror and into God's eyes. That's why truthfulness and passion for God are indivisible. When passion for Him surges through our heart we will love not our lives, even when faced with death (Rev. 12:11). Lying will never be an option! But we can maintain passion for God only in the context of unswerving truthfulness. Passion for God elicits a passion for truth.

Remember Betsy ten Boom telling the gestapo exactly where she and Corrie were hiding the fugitive Jews they kept in their home? The pounding at their door had come unexpectedly, sending terror through everyone sitting around the dining room table eating supper. As Corrie methodically made her way toward the door, everyone scooted the large table aside, lifted the rug underneath, opened the trapdoor below, grabbed their plate and silverware and everything that would give the appearance of a large gathering, and hurriedly stepped down into the darkness. By the time the gestapo agents and soldiers rushed through the opened door, Betsy was standing at the table as if only she, her father, and Corrie had been eating. When the soldiers had thoroughly checked the premises and announced that they found no one, the officer in charge demanded the ten Boom family to tell him where they were hiding the Jews. "I know they are in here. Don't lie to me!" After some strained silence, Betsy finally gave them away. "They are under the table," she said. With that, Corrie almost died of a heart attack.

The officer, however, didn't take Betsy seriously. "Don't make fun of me! Where are they?"

"They are under the table," she repeated, pointing again to the floor under the table. He just scoffed and stomped off.

Corrie later raked her sister over the coals on that one. "Why did you tell them they were under the table? We could have lost everything for sure." But Betsy was adamant. She chose to be truthful and, in doing so, let the Lord be God in the matter. She wasn't going to play His role. Trusting Him no matter what, she would tell the truth, always. Amazingly, when Betsy told the truth to the gestapo officer, God used that very truth to distract his thinking. Unable to imagine the veracity of such a claim, he didn't take her seriously. He mocked her and left.

Is it safe to trust God with the truth? By choosing to be truthful? When He is our passion, we will be convinced of it. But when our physical existence or our fortune or some other passion dominates our imagination, as did David, we likely will not trust Him—not let Him be God. Sadly, it's a role that we'll want to claim.

David's problem was that he didn't trust God to protect and deliver him. He had lost perspective on the past—had lost sight of how God had been with him during his encounters with the bear, with the lion, and with Goliath. As a result he missed the message of what had just transpired in Naioth in Ramah. Now lost in a confusing maze of his current circumstances, he adjusted his ethic to the situation of the moment.

### The Blessed Reminder

David's visit to Nob ends with him asking for a spear or a sword. The only one around was Goliath's, which someone had carefully wrapped in a cloth behind the ephod. It was a symbol of God's power over every giant that anyone could ever face. Evidently David had given this trophy of war as a museum piece for the sanctuary. There in the place of worship it would preserve the memory of the great act of salvation in which God had used him to turn the tide against the Philistines. The Levites carefully kept and tended the sword so that the men and women who came to pray could observe it and renew their faith and trust in God.[11] Ellen White tells us that David's "courage revived as he grasped the sword that he had once used to destroy the champion of the Philistines."[12] And yet, when we read what takes place in the very next episode in his life, we realize that the once-fearless David "now carried both the sword and the mental attitude of Goliath. The weapon had not delivered the giant; neither would it help David."[13]

At Nob David loses some of the beauty of spirit and transparency of character we have come to expect of him. The pressures now upon him show him to be rather human, after all.[14] Human like you and me. Scripture tells it like it is. In the process, inspiration does not present David as a moral model to copy. He is not a person whose actions we should always imitate. In fact, in the company of David we find someone who does it as badly as—or even worse than—we do. "David's isn't an *ideal* life but an *actual* life."[15] But despite everything God doesn't let him go, and David never withdraws from God.

Ellen White tells us that "the pen of inspiration, true to its task, tells us of the sins that overcame Noah, Lot, Moses, Abraham, David, and Solomon, and that even Elijah's strong spirit sank under temptation during his fearful trial. Jonah's disobedience and Israel's idolatry are faithfully recorded. Peter's denial of Christ, the sharp contention of Paul and Barnabas, the failings and infirmities of the prophets and apostles, are all laid bare by the Holy Ghost, who lifts the veil from the human heart. There before us lie the lives of the believers, with all their faults and follies, which are intended as a lesson to all the generations following them. If they had been without foible they would have been more than human, and our sinful natures would despair of ever reaching such a point of excellence. But seeing where they struggled and fell, where they took heart again and conquered through the grace of God, we are encouraged, and led to press over the obstacles that degenerate nature places in our way."[16]

People can quickly succumb to unethical behavior when their faith is on the run. In the heat of the desperate attempt to escape—when we are spiritually and emotionally confused—we can incorrectly assume that our situation is of such a serious nature, such a dire need, that we can accomplish the greatest good only by resorting to a compromising standard of conduct. The ends justify the means! At such times truth and truthfulness are often the first to go. But truthfulness and passion for God are inseparably linked. Truthfulness will always be a quality of authentic faith, even on the run, whether retreating or advancing.

Have you ever lost perspective and become unable to remember God's promises and provisions in your own life? Have you ever taken matters into your own hands and made a mess of things? At such times we can—like David—hurt others. We can cause innocent people to suffer and bring reproach on the name of Christ. It is also times like these that we begin to allow dishonesty to creep into our lives. Our first scheme may be just a little white lie, but our next step leads to a boldfaced one. Before we know it we're in so deep we're feigning something we're not. Soon we've moved from telling lies to living them.[17]

Scripture does not tell us how long it took David to come to grips with lying. Before we finish his fugitive years we'll see this tendency in his life come to full bloom. We catch a glimpse of it in Psalm 34 as he sat alone in the cave of Adullam. Read against the backdrop of what we've learned about David's dishonesty, it is self-explanatory: "Come, my children, and listen to me, and I will teach you to fear the Lord. Do any of you want to live a life that is long and good? Then watch your tongue! Keep your lips from telling lies!" (Ps. 34:11-13, NLT). Evidently he wanted to warn others so they wouldn't make the same mistakes.

How does your life measure up on the truth scale? Check yourself! "Therefore each of you must put off falsehood and speak truthfully to his neighbor, for we are all members of one body" (Eph. 4:25, NIV). Integrity in our interior world will always reflect spiritual passion.

We cannot close this episode without a glimpse of God's incredible grace—grace found in loaves of bread. Famished from his flight, David asked Ahimelech for bread. To be exact, he asked for five loaves. His request strikes a familiar chord to those acquainted with Scripture and sensitive to the links between David and Christ. Christ fed the multitudes with five loaves of bread (Matt. 14:19). David requested of Ahimelech, "Give me five loaves of bread, or anything else you have" (1 Sam. 21:3, NLT). When Christ sent the disciples to search for food to feed the hungry multitude, they could find only five loaves. For David, no bread could be found except holy bread, the bread of the presence placed before the Lord in the tabernacle (verse 6). Perhaps God had a point to make with the five loaves. God might have purposely used the bread of the presence to feed David because such bread symbolized God's everlasting covenant with His people (Lev. 24:5-9). He might have wanted to symbolize too His gracious provision through David's fugitive years.

The Hebrew term for presence is *paneh,* which means "countenance, presence, or face." The bread of presence reminded God's people of the pledge of His presence—something David desperately needed as his spiritual passion withered further in the wake of his untruthfulness. The Lord was doing more with the bread at Nob than feeding David's hungry stomach. I believe God pledged His presence to David and promised to be his complete sustainer. As David ate those five loaves, the Spirit of God would remind him of God's covenant presence and covenant provision. Maybe that's why Christ focused on mercy rather than condemnation when He made reference to David's eating this holy bread (Matt. 12:1-8). One greater than the holy bread of the tabernacle was there. How else could his spiritual passion be restored? Or ours!

---

[1] Ellen G. White, *Patriarchs and Prophets*, p. 654.

[2] Gene A. Getz, *David: Seeking God Faithfully*, p. 90. See White, *Patriarchs and Prophets*, p. 653.

[3] White, *Patriarchs and Prophets*, p. 654.

[4] *Ibid.*

[5] *Ibid.*, p. 656.

[6] Keith Kaynor, *When God Chooses: The Life of David*, p. 76.

[7] White, *Patriarchs and Prophets*, p. 656.

[8] Kaynor, p. 79. (Italics supplied.)

[9] *Ibid.*, p. 80.

[10] White, *Patriarchs and Prophets*, p. 656.

[11] Eugene H. Peterson, *Leap Over a Wall*, pp. 63, 64.

[12] White, *Patriarchs and Prophets*, p. 656.

[13] Kaynor, p. 78.

[14] *Ibid.*, p. 75.

[15] Peterson, p. 62.

[16] White, *Testimonies for the Church* (Mountain View, Calif.: Pacific Press Pub. Assn., 1948), vol. 4, p. 12.

[17] Getz, p. 97.

4

# FINDING YOUR CAVE
# WHEN YOU'VE ACTED INSANE

## I Samuel 21:10–22:2

She would hear imaginary voices and argue angrily with them or hurl ketchup bottles through glass windows at faces she thought she saw. Other times she could sit for hours with a far-off, almost troubled look on her face, fidgeting with her fingers and jerking nervously. Or pace back and forth in the house muttering thunderous curses and bizarre statements. Sometimes she appeared wild-eyed and greatly agitated. At such times she could get quite noisy. Whenever she wasn't on her medication, she was unruly and difficult to handle.

I loved my grandma, and have many fond memories of her giving me a woodpecker kiss (pucker your lips softly on a child's cheek and draw in air ever so slightly but steady until there's a rhythmic pecking sound—they like it!). She would walk me around on her feet when I was little. At breakfast she would fix buckwheat pancakes so big that they hung over the edges of a 12-inch plate and served them with eggs sunny-side up and fresh fried trout. I remember too the fascinating stories she'd tell and the zany folk songs she would sing—such as "Mrs. Murphy's Chowder" or "I'm My Own Grandpa." And how the house would literally shudder when she played hoedown music on her pearl-laden violin, singing out the dance calls with her raspy voice, dancing at the same time (she was a heavy woman). Of course there were the unforgettable summers I spent with her and Grandpa on the family farm in northern Pennsylvania.

But sometimes being around Grandma was just plain frightening. Her schizophrenia could make her downright spooky if you were a kid. Her gravelly, almost male voice (the result of years of chain-smoking) could scare the wits out of you. Her abnormal behavior would give you the distinct feeling that she was really out of it—loony. That she was someone to avoid. At times you instinctively wanted to distance yourself from her. You did not want to be around her, nor did you want her around. And you did not want anyone outside the family to know about her. Sometimes, as kids, we had detached ourselves to the place where we said insensitive things about Grandma or made jokes about her. My own sons have memories of unexpected meetings with their great-grandma when, as any grandchild would do, they wandered around grandma's house exploring and all of a sudden came across their great-grandma in the corner of a darkened room. Seeing her in dim light—unkept hair and darkened eyes behind thick glasses, suddenly calling to them or standing up in the shadows—could spook anyone.

David unnerved the Philistines when he feigned madness. After seeing Doeg at Nob, David ran some 23 miles southwest to Gath (1 Sam. 21:10). Gath was Goliath's birthplace. It was also the headquarters for the Philistine people. King Achish was in power at the time and had his court there. David approached Achish, hoping for asylum because Saul was now their mutual enemy. Can you imagine it? Of all people, here was David at Gath, of all places, looking for the Philistine king! But fear and unbelief sometimes cause us to become reckless. We can do some pretty stupid things when fear fuels us and we have taken our eyes away from God.

I'm not sure what David was thinking, but the people in Gath instantly recognized him. Maybe they saw Goliath's sword hanging on his belt and put two and two together. Whatever the explanation, his arrival in the city immediately aroused suspicions. David's presence made Achish's servants particularly uneasy. Was he looking for trouble? Was his sudden appearance some kind of ruse? David's hands had been soaked with Philistine blood. His fortunes had come at the expense of many bereaved hearts and homes throughout the Philistine confederacy.[1] They were quite aware of his status as a Hebrew folk hero celebrated with song and dance.[2]

"Is this not David the king of the land?" they asked one another. "Did they not sing of this one as they danced, saying, 'Saul has slain his thousands, and David his ten thousands'?" (1 Sam. 21:11, NASB).

So the authorities immediately labeled David persona non grata and placed him in protective custody while they debated his fate (see the inscription at the beginning of Psalm 56—"A Mikhtam of David, when the Philistines seized him in Gath").[3]

In custody and overhearing the Philistine reaction, David realized that his life was as much at risk in the royal court of Gath as it was in the royal court of Gibeah. Physically and emotionally exhausted, David was frightened by the situation. He "took these words to heart and greatly feared Achish king of Gath" (verse 12, NASB). But David was a quick thinker. Feigning insanity, he went around damaging public property by scratching marks on the doors of the gate. Probably they involved writing nonsensical graffiti or symbols associated with cultic curses. David also let saliva run down his beard (verse 13). We can only imagine other bizarre behaviors he might have employed, such as staring eyes, trembling limbs, matted hair, torn clothes, crazy utterances, perhaps even soiling himself.

Although we may wonder why the men of Gath didn't kill David on the spot, he knew the pagan people of his day. They were terrified of an insane person and far too superstitious to harm one. The ancient world regarded insanity as an indication that the gods were inhabiting a human body. Erratic behavior supposedly indicated divine presence, or at least a demon who could play havoc from the next existence.[4] So when David's bizarre conduct convinced the Philistines that he was insane, they didn't harm him. Think about it. Wouldn't you be a bit superstitious if you saw him scratching on the gate, saliva dribbling down his beard, looking insane—and yet carrying Goliath's sword? You would put two and two together and think to yourself, *Hey, the gods are with this guy. While he may be crazy, he's got Goliath's sword. We better leave him alone. He has secret powers.* So the men of Gath didn't kill David. His little theatrical production had spooked them.

But while their superstition kept them from permanently imprisoning or executing him, it wouldn't necessarily make them desire his presence. The fact is, they didn't want anything to do with David. So we encounter the general demeaning of the mentally ill that was also part of Philistine culture. Hence Achish's reaction—one of those wonderful lines that show Scripture is not only the Word of God but the greatest literature you can find—"Look! The man is crazy! Why bring him to me? Am I so short of madmen that you have to bring this fellow here to carry on like this in front of me?" (see verses 14, 15). Gath didn't need any more mentally disturbed people.[5]

Anyway, acting insane worked. David was quick on his feet, a creative and shrewd protagonist in a dangerously awkward situation. He certainly wasn't short on personality, was he? The problem, though, was that he was acting (literally) for his life. He was operating on the strength of his wits, on his own resources. And it would only leave him further exhausted. Can you imagine the adrenaline rush in a moment like that? Medically, the adrenaline-filled body can't survive for long. Prolonged exposure to the hormone causes major psychological and physiological problems. Spiritually, the adrenaline-filled spirit lasts for a moment—then dies. The stress and adrenaline cause people to spiral down the passion tube, leaving them emotionally and spiritually exhausted.

Because of their superstition, the people of Gath eventually allowed this Israelite madman to come and go as he wished. When the timing was right, David escaped to the cave of Adullam, some 10 miles to the east (1 Sam. 22:1).

### Feeling Like an Idiot

When I was in grade school one of my best friends had epilepsy. As long as Stephen took his medicine he did all right. Even then, though, seizures could overwhelm him unexpectedly. I remember vividly some of those frenzied and confusing moments when he would tremble and drool. His sweat would soak his clothing, or he might soil his pants. A frightened wild stare would fill his eyes. Then exhaustion would overtake him when the seizure ended. Mostly I remember his reaction afterward. Extremely self-conscious, he felt helpless, embarrassed, abnormal, and ashamed. He just wanted to disappear. If a person has these kinds of reactions when they are not able to control the situation, how do you think they feel when they could have but didn't? How does anyone feel when they have acted the fool in full broad daylight?

By the time David reached the cave of Adullam he was in pretty bad condition inside. He had been merely acting like an idiot at Gath. Now he felt like a real one. How humiliating to have to pretend madness by scribbling on the walls and letting saliva dribble over into his beard! What an extremely undignified moment for someone who had been anointed by the Spirit of God and had done so many mighty things![6] Before Gath David had "displayed noble traits of character, and his moral worth had won him favor with the people; but as trial came upon him," it shook his faith, "and human weakness appeared."[7] Now David didn't like what he saw in himself. He could only wonder inside, *How in the world did I ever get here?* It was the lowest moment of his life. In the downward swirl of events he had lost his self-respect. Going from national hero to madman, David had fallen from the pinnacle of success to the depths of disgrace. Even his enemies had discarded him. It would be easy to imagine that God had abandoned him as well. *What a fool,* he thought to himself. *What a fool!*

Talk about loss of passion! How can you have passion for anything when you have lost self-respect? When you've acted like an idiot, feelings of failure and personal embarrassment, of self-doubt and negativism, paralyze any possibility of spiritual passion. It is all that one can do to deal with self, let alone God.

As David crawled into the cave of Adullam, its darkness matched the gloom that had captured his soul. If you want to know how David really felt, just read the lament he composed about it. The descriptive line at the beginning of many of the psalms gives us their author and their context. The opening words of Psalm 142 read: "A maskil of David, when he was in the cave. A prayer."

"I cry out loudly to [Yahweh],
    loudly I plead with [Yahweh] for mercy.
I spill out all my complaints before him,
    and spell out my troubles in detail:
As I sink in despair, my spirit ebbing away,
    you know how I'm feeling,
Know the danger I'm in,
    the traps hidden in my path.
Look right, look left—

there's not a soul that cares what happens!
I'm up against it, with no exit—
   bereft, left alone.
I cry out, [Yahweh], call out:
   'You're my last chance, my only hope for life!'
Oh listen, please listen;
   I've never been this low.
Rescue me from those who are hunting me down;
   I'm no match for them.
Get me out of this dungeon
   so I can thank you in public.
Your people will form a circle around me
   and you'll bring me showers of blessing!"
                              —Psalm 142:1-7, Message

Can you imagine the mixture of fear, rage, abandonment, and bewilderment David must have experienced while hiding in that cave? "I don't know of a soul on earth who cares for my soul. I am brought very low. I've never been this low. Get me out of this dungeon. Deliver me, Lord." Overwhelmed, he felt vulnerable and depressed. Can you sense the loneliness of that desolate spot? Can you feel his despair? How worthless he felt? How useless, mistreated, and alone? So far away from God? David felt like an idiot because he had acted like one. That is why he was in that dark godforsaken cave, tucked away in some remote crevice of a mountain. The cave's name was fitting: Adullam, a word meaning "sealed-off place." But it was just what David wanted—to seal himself away so that no one could see.

Had 1 Samuel 22 been our only text on this dispirited moment in David's life, we would never have known some of what he experienced. Thankfully, God inspired him to write his feelings. As a result, they can help us when we ourselves have acted like an idiot. Most of us want to crawl into a hole and die after some of the irrational and foolish things we have said or done or allowed ourselves to get into. When we've acted insane we feel overwhelmed, worthless, and useless. At such moments of darkness we often ask ourselves, "How in the world did I get here?" Like David, we become depressed, broken, and disgraced. We are only a failure living in a cave of discouragement, withdrawal, and loneliness. Self-respect is gone, and so is spiritual passion.

Most of the time when we have played the fool—when we crawl into our cave to lick our wounds—we prefer to avoid others. Sometimes we just cannot stand to be with people. We hate to admit it publicly—in fact, we usually do not—and I have a feeling that at this moment of confusion and embarrassment David wanted nobody around. If he wasn't worth anything to himself, he surely could not see how he would be of value to anybody else.[8]

But God had other thoughts. David did not want his family, but God brought them anyway. When his brothers and his father's household heard how he had holed himself up in the cave of Adullam, they went down to be with him there. They crawled right into that dark cave with him (1 Sam. 22:1). When he was at rock bottom and wanted to be alone, God knew he needed people, especially his family.

David's family were not the only ones who joined him. Other hurting people showed up and crowded into the cave with him. "Everyone who was in distress, and everyone who was in debt, and everyone who was discontented gathered to him; and he became captain over them. Now there were about four hundred men with him" (verse 2, NASB). Did you catch the makeup of this motley crew?—everyone who was in distress, in debt, or discontented. They were the three Ds. Those who were under pressure and whose lives were filled with trouble. Those who couldn't pay their bills—most likely the poor. And those who had a bitter spirit because they had been wronged and mistreated or suffered great loss, no doubt feeling disenfranchised from Saul's world.[9]

It probably was not easy at first to have family around. After all, David had tasted the bitterness of distrust on the part of all his own brothers as well as the specific anger of his older brother. But the support and harmony that they now offered brought joy to the fugitive's heart.[10] Then when all those other malcontents showed up, David probably did not relish that either. The last thing you want when you're down and out is to be among a bunch of losers. But sometimes when you see others who have "been there; endured that!" it gives you perspective and calls you out of yourself to build those others up. God uses the support of others, even the comradery of brokenness, to restore spiritual passion. As Psalm 142 exclaims: "Your people will form a circle around me and you'll bring me showers of blessing!" (verse 7, Message). The circle of others and the showers of blessing have an inseparable link. When we allow ourselves to be so surrounded, spiritual passion has a chance to flourish again.

## Finding Dignity, Grace, and Power

Where do you turn when the bottom drops out of your life? Who will offer you help when you face a personally embarrassing issue or you are spiritually drained down even to the loss of self-respect? Psalm 142 reveals how David survived. In the psalm he still wanted God no matter how he felt. No matter how low he had fallen or how much of a fool he had been. Even when stripped of self-respect, David still wanted God. "You're my last chance, my only hope for life!" he cries (verse 5, Message).

When unfair treatment and difficult circumstance overwhelmed him or he felt drained of spiritual passion or felt the loss of self-respect, he prayed. No, he cried out loud. We can imagine him sobbing in the cave. Sobbing his heart out to God in the darkness. There he poured out his complaint to the Lord. He told God about his troubles—what was hurting him. But David did not just pour out his emotion; he also rehearsed his trust in God. "When my spirit grows faint within me," he sobbed, "it is you who know my way" (verse 3, NIV). "You alone know the way I should turn" (NLT). By now he was so exhausted that he feared he could no longer stay alert to the snares his enemies were continually setting for him. His prayer was a reminder to himself: "God knows my way. He knows what is happening. He knows what I should do next. Where I should go. God knows my way." David longed for divine presence.

The desperate fugitive composed two other psalms during this dark period of depression and despair—Psalms 57 and 34. We do not know for sure in what order he wrote the three psalms, but looking at his experience, they seem to fit in reverse order.[11] The intensity of despair depicted in Psalm 142 suggests that it likely emerged first, when David was at his greatest despair, perhaps prostrate on his face. The language of Psalm 57, however, seems to indicate an in-between experience in which he still experienced emotional trauma, but felt encouraged, perhaps looking upward on his knees. Here we find David telling himself deep down inside to focus on God rather than on himself and his discouraging circumstances. "Wake up, my soul!" he says. Listen:

"Be exalted, O God, above the highest heavens!
May your glory shine over all the earth.
My enemies have set a trap for me.
I am weary from distress.
They have dug a deep pit in my path,
but they themselves have fallen into it. *Interlude*
My heart is confident in you, O God;
no wonder I can sing your praises!
Wake up, my soul!
Wake up, O harp and lyre!
I will waken the dawn with my song.
I will thank you, Lord, in front of all the people.
I will sing your praises among the nations.
For your unfailing love is as high as the heavens.
Your faithfulness reaches to the clouds.
Be exalted, O God, above the highest heavens.
May your glory shine over all the earth."
—Psalm 57:5-11, NLT

Psalm 34 reveals the most optimism and faith. David is back, as it were, on his feet. He is free of fear, and shame no longer darkens his face. Protecting angels hover near. Confidence that God has seen and heard fills him. Forgiveness is real! Again listen:

"I prayed to the Lord, and he answered me,
freeing me from all my fears.
Those who look to him for help will be radiant with joy;
no shadow of shame will darken their faces.
I cried out to the Lord in my suffering, and he heard me.
He set me free from all my fears.
For the angel of the Lord guards all who fear him,
and he rescues them. . . .
The eyes of the Lord watch over those who do right;
his ears are open to their cries for help. . . .
The Lord hears his people when they call to him for help.
He rescues them from all their troubles.
The Lord is close to the brokenhearted;

> he rescues those who are crushed in spirit.
> The righteous face many troubles,
>> but the Lord rescues them from each and every one. . . .
> But the Lord will redeem those who serve him.
> Everyone who trusts in him will be freely pardoned."
>> —Psalm 34:4-22, NLT

Together these psalms show us how David emerged from the cave of Adullam spiritually revived, confident in God, and sensing His presence and power.[12] His spiritual passion had been restored—for a while, at least.

Rather than allowing his failures to hold him captive, David turned to God. Ceasing to wallow in self-pity, he directed his gaze heavenward. And instead of repeating old patterns, he refocused his attitudes and behavior.[13] He opened his heart to accept the sympathy and affection of his family. Then he reached out to the 400 misfits who had crawled into the cave with him and instilled in them order and discipline, character and direction. That motley crew became his mighty men in battle and, later, some would become his cabinet when he took office.

How did this change take place? It came because David hurt enough to admit his need and was humble enough to lean once again on God.[14] He was willing to let others minister to him and selfless enough to reach out to others who were also hurting.

Have you been acting insane and feeling like an idiot? Where do you turn when your life collapses? Or when you face an embarrassing—perhaps even scandalous—issue? Life hits rock bottom—so what do you do now? How do you feel forgiven when you've played the fool?

David points the way to renewal. Just as his flight to Israel's cave of Adullam was also a return to spiritual health, our very own cave can become a moment of renewal—if we remain humble, are honest with ourselves and the Lord, keep praying, and trust in God.

Ellen White tells us that "every failure on the part of the children of God is due to their lack of faith. When shadows encompass the soul, when we want light and guidance, we must look up; there is light beyond the darkness."[15]

Once more listen to the light David found in his darkness:

> "The eyes of the Lord watch over those who do right;
>> his ears are open to their cries for help. . . .

The Lord hears his people when they call to him for help.
He rescues them from all their troubles.
The Lord is close to the brokenhearted;
    he rescues those who are crushed in spirit.
The righteous face many troubles,
    but the Lord rescues them from each and every one. . . .
But the Lord will redeem those who serve him.
Everyone who trusts in him will be freely pardoned."

Take a moment to think through the reason you find yourself submerged in such dark feelings and dismal outlook. Is it something from your recent past? Something that you feel angry about or that has damaged the relationship between yourself and another person? Let David's story pull you toward God. Restore your spiritual passion by fixing your gaze on Him, filling your mouth with praise and the self-talk of your interior world with words from these psalms.

One truth I take from David's tragic crash in the cave is that faith on the run does not mean passion for God is necessarily gone. Yes, spiritual passion may plummet in the wake of our confusion and compromise. God's immediate care and concern may seem blurred and out of focus. We may take things into our own hands—scheming, conniving, lying, running in fear, falling flat on our face, descending into a pit of discouragement and depression. And yet, in our heart of hearts, deep within our troubled and emotionally raw soul, we instinctively turn to God. Crying out to Him, we desperately seek Him. Prayer forms on our lips, even if it's just a fleeting thought between waves of exhausting pain. In the end, it is those who know that they can do nothing without God's help who have passion for God. Be encouraged!

---

[1] Theodore H. Epp, *A Man After the Heart of God*, p. 67.
[2] Robert D. Bergen, *1, 2 Samuel*, p. 223.
[3] Keith Kaynor, *When God Chooses: The Life of David*, p. 84.
[4] *Ibid.* See also Robert P. Gordon, *I and II Samuel: A Commentary* (Grand Rapids: Zonderman Pub. Assn., 1999), p. 172, and Ralph W. Klein, *1 Samuel* (Nashville: Nelson Reference and Electronic Publishing, 1983), p. 217.
[5] Klein, *1 Samuel*, p. 217.
[6] Alan Redpath, *The Making of a Man of God: Study in the Life of David* (Grand Rapids: Fleming H. Revell, 1994), p. 72.
[7] Ellen G. White, *Patriarchs and Prophets*, pp. 656, 657.
[8] C. R. Swindoll, *David: A Man of Passion and Destiny*, pp. 73, 74.

[9] Klein, *1 Samuel,* pp. 222, 223.
[10] White, *Patriarchs and Prophets,* p. 658.
[11] Swindoll, p. 75.
[12] Gene Getz, *David: Seeking God Faithfully,* p. 101.
[13] *Ibid.,* p. 106.
[14] Swindoll, pp. 77, 78.
[15] White, *Patriarchs and Prophets,* p. 657.

5

# BETRAYAL IN THE WIRELESSZONE

## I Samuel 23:1-14

We were seated across from one another while eating breakfast during a ministerial retreat. She and her husband were new to the conference pastoral team where I worked. They ministered in Michigan's upper peninsula, a good day's drive from the lower southwest corner where I pastored. It was our first contact and quite unplanned. We just happened to wind up at the same table together. She had no idea who I was, and I did not know who she was. But that didn't keep her from asking questions. Lots of them. Now, I'm phlegmatic. Making conversation over breakfast even with people that I do know is work, unless I'm fully awake—which I didn't happen to be right then. That morning I would have been satisfied with the usual "Good morning. My name is Larry Lichtenwalter. And yours? Where did you say you were pastoring? Nice day. Great waffles." I wanted to eat and get back to my room for something I was working on, but she kept asking questions. Wanting not to appear impolite or unsociable (which I was), I responded, usually, though, with one-word answers.

Learning my name did not seem to mean that much to her, but when I finally revealed where I pastored, she became quite enthusiastic about the church-based counseling ministry our pastoral staff provides. Evidently it had made a drastic difference in one woman's life, someone in their congregation. She just had to tell me!

A lot of our on-staff counselor's work is confidential. I have no idea whom she sees. Nor am I acquainted with the specific needs or issues that she deals with in their lives. Now, suddenly I was learning about a hurting woman who had come all the way down from the Upper Peninsula to our church in order to receive concentrated ministry from our counselor for nearly two weeks. I did not learn the woman's name, nor do I know whose home she stayed in while we ministered to her. In fact, I did not even know it had taken place. But now I was hearing that she had come to us deeply hurting and quite dysfunctional in both her personal and social life. Yet after two weeks of caring Christian counseling, she returned home with emotional healing as well as some practical new spiritual and emotional insights (tools, if you will) to keep growing. Praise God!

What perked my ears was hearing about this woman's involvement in their little Upper Peninsula congregation. Almost overnight she had gone from being detached and self-oriented to engaged and other-oriented. This once-hurting woman had emerged as a vibrant new leader using her spiritual gifts to minister to others and make a difference in their lives. The emotional healing that had taken place in her life had freed her to help others.

When we are consumed with our own problems, we do not have the emotional or spiritual resources to think about others or meet their needs. Hurting people not only injure others; they are often unable even to sense when others are in pain. Usually they do not have the emotional or spiritual resources to aid someone else even if they wanted to. When we have acted insane and feel like an idiot, we usually do not have much to give to others. Spiritual passion is usually exhausted. But when, through God's grace, our spiritual and emotional well-being revives and we experience inner healing, not only can we recognize the needs of others, but they become important to us as well. We not only *can* make a difference; we *want* to. That is what my congregation's church-based counseling ministry is all about. It seeks to bring spiritual and emotional well-being to hurting people so that God can use them to help some other aching heart. Emotional healing frees us to help others. It liberates us to discover our spiritual gifts and then to employ them to mend broken people. Since we are no longer absorbed with ourselves and emotionally paralyzed, our spiritual passion overflows toward others.

This was David's experience in the cave of Adullam. In a downward swirl of events he had lost his job, his wife, his home, his most trusted counselor (Samuel), his closest friend (Jonathan), and finally his self-respect. Feeling like an idiot, he had crawled into the isolated cave. Emotionally drained, he focused on self and wallowed in deep depression. He had little if anything to give anyone else. In fact, he needed the support of his family. He required the group therapy that the 400 hurting people provided when they crawled into the dark cave along with him. David needed to connect with God again.

There in the cave of Adullam, David experienced emotional and spiritual renewal (see Ps. 142, 56, 34, and 57). In addition, as he both received support from, and reached out as a leader to, the 400 hurting people who joined him in the cave, they provided him with resources for accomplishing things he could not do on his own. So when news reached him that the Philistines were raiding the town of Keilah, he immediately felt responsible to do what he could to help. "Then they told David, saying, 'Behold, the Philistines are fighting against Keilah and are plundering the threshing floors.' So David inquired of the Lord, saying, 'Shall I go and attack these Philistines?'" (1 Sam. 23:1, 2, NASB). He was no longer so engrossed with his own problems that he forgot or overlooked those of his own Israelite people.[1] Interestingly, at this very time Saul too was preoccupied with jealousy and revenge. Because of his emotional dysfunction, he was either neglecting or bruising those around him.[2] With both Saul and David caught up in their own emotional pain or dysfunction, the Philistines were having a party. That's how the devil works! In the midst of our dysfunction, the devil often has a heyday in the lives of those around us.

But healed people heal people! They want to help, to make a difference. When spiritual passion is on the rise, so is a passion to help.

Keilah was a fortified city less than three miles south of the cave of Adullam. Located in an agriculturally rich region, it was somewhat isolated from other Israelite cities. The farmers had just harvested their crops and brought the grain to the threshing floors, creating an attractive and vulnerable target for Philistine plunderers who ranged the country like predatory animals. Threshing floors would be the logical thing to attack because the raiders could immediately use grain and the sites were only lightly defended. In addition, the loss of the crop would bring great hardship to the poor Israelite peasants.

David faced a dilemma. Helping the people of Keilah meant that he would be putting himself at risk. Not only would the Philistines have superior armaments and greater numbers, but going after them would call attention to his whereabouts. Also he and his men could get caught in a crossfire. While they fought the Philistines Saul and his army could show up from behind, pinching them in between.[3] Should he defend his fellow Israelites and thereby put himself and his men at greater risk?

In that difficult situation David did something characteristic of a man who had not yet lost his passion for God. He prayed for guidance. "Shall I go and attack these Philistines?" he asked. "Go and attack the Philistines and deliver Keilah," came the answer (verse 2, NASB). The method David used to discern God's will is unknown. Perhaps the prophet Gad was part of the equation. God had sent him to David to tell him to get out of the cave and to return to Judah (1 Sam. 22:5). Gad would be with David for the next 60 years and in the end became one of his biographers. Whatever David's method of discerning the Lord's will, it was not good enough for his men. They were not enthusiastic about taking on the Philistines. To them, the idea of going up against an army with superior armaments and greater numbers did not seem divinely inspired. "We're afraid even here in Judah," they exclaimed. "We certainly don't want to go to Keilah to fight the whole Philistine army!" (1 Sam 23:3, NLT). So David prayed again. And once again God told him to attack the Philistines and save Keilah. So David and his men fought the Philistines and rescued the people of Keilah (verses 4-6).

I invite you to catch one of the subtle themes running through this episode—a theme that demonstrates David's spiritual and emotional renewal. He did not run off on his own again, nor did he take matters into his own hand. His downward slide from faith to fear had bottomed out in the cave of Adullam. Once again David was willing to wait for the Lord's leading and divine empowerment. Fear was no longer his overriding passion. Now he had renewed trust in God and a passionate concern for his endangered fellow people. As a fugitive, David was learning an important principle of spiritual passion—the link between courage and waiting. It was something he would sing about later: "Wait patiently for the Lord. Be strong and let your heart be bold. Yes, wait patiently for the Lord" (Ps. 27:14, paraphrase).

It is so much easier to lie down and die, run to friends, flee for your life, or feign madness than to wait. But waiting is the true posture of passion for the Lord. Those that wait for God will not be long without the God for whom they rest in anticipation. Waiting involves the very essence of a person's being, their soul *(nephesh)*: "I wait for the Lord, my soul waits, and in his word I put my hope." Those who do so in true faith find themselves renewed in strength so that they can continue to serve the Lord while looking for His saving work (Isa. 40:31). The Hebrew language linked waiting with hope, often using the same word to mean both. Ultimately, waiting is on God, who is our hope: "And now, Lord, for what do I wait? My hope is in You" (Ps. 39:7, NASB). Such waiting means the stilling of the soul. "My soul," David declares, "wait in silence for God only, for my hope is from Him" (Ps. 62:5, NASB). Waiting is the true posture of passion for God. Those who have passion for God wait. And those who wait have passion for God.

Have you ever moved too quickly in a direction you believed that God was sending you and later realized you were hasty and might have misunderstood His leading? That maybe it wasn't God at all that you were following, just your own will becoming so real in your thinking that it felt as if God were speaking? That can happen when we are eager to restore lost spiritual passion. Especially when, as with David, we have done some really stupid things but now want to be passionate for God again. In our zeal things may not be as clear as we think. Earlier David was quick to move (literally run for his life) on his own without seeking God's guidance, without waiting for a word from the Lord, and without trusting His protecting providence. Now, perhaps, he is again tempted to move too quickly.

Not surprisingly, his men were not as enthusiastic as he was about saving Keilah. Their resistance provided a healthy check to David's risky proposition. His response reminds us that doubting God and doubting that we fully understood God are two different things.[4] Rather than shaming his men for questioning the word he had received from the Lord, David went back to God and reconfirmed His direction. He did not ask a second time because He doubted God, but because he needed to be certain that he understood correctly. In the same way, at times you or I might ask God to reconfirm His direction—not because we challenge His Word, but because we question our own understanding. To doubt God in the face of clear direction is disobedience, but to double-check our understanding and interpretation of His will is prudent. It is part of waiting, being still enough inside until we can hear His voice above our own. Waiting is not necessarily an element of time, it may be a matter of distinguishing the voice of the Lord from other voices. Some musicians can tell if a specific member of a quartet or choir has missed a note or sounded a wrong note. This calls for a carefully trained ear, the very thing the Lord wants us to have in the spiritual realm.[5]

## Betrayal in the WirelessZone

As part of the information technology provided for its students, Andrews University introduced wireless computing at select sites on its campus marked WirelessZone. WirelessZones allow you to connect your laptop computer to the campus network without the need of plugging into a wall jack. You are free to roam within the zones without the worry of losing your connection. Imagine the possibilities. You can check your e-mail during lunch at the café. Research the Web site during class rather than listen to the teacher. Or chat with a friend on the other side of the world while you sit at a bench during a sunny spring day. It is all possible with wireless computing. You cannot see, touch, or hear WirelessZones—but they are there, connecting your computer to a vast array of resources and opportunities. All you have to do is look for the special green diamonds posted around campus alerting you to the presence of a WirelessZone. As the WirelessZone slogan says: "Unplug and get connected!"

David got connected in a wilderness WirelessZone. "When Abiathar son of Ahimelech fled to David at Keilah, he came down with an ephod in his hand" (1 Sam. 23:6, NRSV). Abiathar was the sole survivor of the Nob massacre. With the death of his father, Ahimelech, he was now Israel's new high priest, and for the next 50 years he would be of great help to David. Somehow during the confusion of that brutal slaughter at Nob Abiathar was able to slip away with the ephod. The ephod was a treasured sacred garment that made direct communication with God possible (1 Sam. 22:20-23). A breastplate worn by the high priest, it had two stones attached to it called the Urim and Thummim. The Hebrew words mean "lights" and "perfection." We don't know exactly how they worked, but they perhaps glowed in response to "yes" and "no" questions addressed to God by the high priest. Like a wireless network card in a laptop, they allowed instant free access to God anywhere. What a WirelessZone! Can you imagine? Wherever the high priest went he had those two stones that flickered on and off, giving him answers to life's vital questions. When the ephod showed up on the scene, David immediately connected.

The point of all this is that he had ready access to God.[6] The deficiencies and questions that plagued David's previous efforts to know the divine would get dealt with in a convincing way. He was once again relying on the Lord. His successful experience in communicating with the Lord demonstrates the vitality of his renewed relationship with God. Between the prophet Gad and the high priest Abiathar with the sacred ephod David was able at any moment to know the divine will![7] It contrasts starkly with Saul's conspicuous failure to establish a link with God. While David had easy and extended access to God, Saul did not. "When Saul inquired of the Lord, the Lord did not answer him, either by dreams or by Urim or by the prophets" (1 Sam. 28:6, NKJV). Israel's first king was a man who, no matter how he prayed, received no answer from God. Why? He had no passion for the Lord. His heart was not right toward Him. "If I regard wickedness in my heart, the Lord will not hear" (Ps. 66:18, NASB). Only a humble heart and a conscious turning from sin will result in God hearing from heaven (2 Chron. 7:14).

Not only did he have no connection with or answer from God; Saul had difficulty interpreting circumstances. When he heard that David had come to Keilah, he said, "God has delivered him into my hand, for he shut himself in by entering a city with double gates and bars" (1 Sam. 23:7, NASB). What strange interpretations one can place on circumstances when one is not right with God![8] If we do not wholly give our wills over to the Lord, we are bound to misinterpret the situations surrounding us.[9] While we may be in the WirelessZone we do not have what it takes to connect with God, and thus we lack moral or spiritual discernment.

While David triumphantly entered Keilah, his mind was still busy looking for a way of escape in case of an emergency. The walled city could prove a trap. He knew that someone would soon tell Saul that he was in it. Could he count on the people there to support him now that he had literally saved their city, possibly even their lives? How could he know for sure if they would be sufficiently grateful to defend him against Saul? Fugitives are always on the watch. Uncertainty and mistrust involuntarily haunt their subconscious, driving them to consider all options or contingencies.

When Saul learned that David had rescued the inhabitants of Keilah, the king thought for sure that he had finally cornered his prey in a walled city. God was on his side, he concluded as he mobilized his entire army to march to Keilah and attack David and his men. So when reports of Saul's massive conscription order reached David (verses 8, 9), he told Abiathar the priest to bring the ephod and ask the Lord what he should do. His prayer was humble, yet pointed: "O Lord, God of Israel, I have heard that Saul is planning to come and destroy Keilah because I am here. Will the men of Keilah surrender me to him? And will Saul actually come as I have heard? O Lord, God of Israel, please tell me" (verses 10, 11, NLT). "And the Lord said, 'He will come.' "Again David asked, 'Will these men of Keilah really betray me and my men to Saul?' And the Lord replied, 'Yes, they will betray you'" (verses 11, 12, NLT). Twice David inquired whether he would be betrayed. Twice the ephod stones radiated their disappointing answer—"They will betray you."

At that moment David learned a painful, bitter lesson. Sometimes the very people you help betray you. The Keilahites owed David their well-being, their material possessions, and probably even their lives. But when the rubber hit the road, they would look out for themselves. They had no loyalty to David. Maybe they had Nob in mind when they considered their options. But it didn't matter. At bottom they were cowardly and ungrateful townspeople who would not hesitate to save themselves by surrendering their deliverer if forced to choose between the king and a fugitive. Here David learned that he needed to be realistic about human nature. It is fickle, self-serving, ungrateful. He could not set his expectations too high lest he be disappointed. And he discovered too how to be unselfish in dealing with ungrateful people deeply indebted to him.

David was too gracious to place the people of Keilah in a position of having to decide between himself and Saul. Quietly he packed his bags, gathered his troops, and left town. He traveled to some of his own kinsmen in Ziph but soon found them unfaithful as well. The men of Ziph went to Saul in Gibeah and betrayed David to him. "We know where David is hiding," they said. "He is in the strongholds of Horesh on the hill of Hakilah, which is in the southern part of Jeshimon" (verse 19, NLT).

It is heartbreaking to discover that our foes are sometimes those whom we have either helped significantly or are related to us closely in some way (relative, work associate, friend, colleague).[10] How often we have a problem with loyalties and gratefulness. Sometimes the very people we aid are the ones who turn against us. Being let down never feels good. When we find ourselves betrayed repeatedly, we risk becoming paranoid and cynical. Soon convincing ourselves that no one can be trusted—even God—we can turn our back on trust itself. Such moments try spiritual passion, requiring a connection with God that overrides one's plummeting emotional energy.

## The Rock of Escape

Years ago I caught a flying squirrel. I had a bluebird house nailed to a tree across the yard just at the edge of the woods. Since bluebirds prefer a more open environment, none of them took up the offer. That didn't keep me, though, from opening the hinged side every once in a while to double-check. On one of those occasions I gently pulled open the side panel and caught the quick exit of a little furry animal out the birdhouse door. It happened so fast that it took me a moment to realize what I had just seen. "That was a flying squirrel," I concluded. I hadn't seen one since I was a boy, when I had one as a pet. It never crossed my mind that they lived near my Michigan home. My decision was instant. "If this is his nest, he'll be back, and he'll be mine before long." An hour or so later I returned to the bluebird house with a quart-sized canning jar in my hand. After placing the opening of the jar over the door of the birdhouse, I slowly opened the side panel just a wee crack, shoving a small stick through the opening. In an instant, the furry little critter bolted out the birdhouse door and into my waiting jar. Quickly I slid the jar down the side of the birdhouse, trapping him inside. It took only a moment to slide the lid on. Just like that I had my flying squirrel firmly in hand. He was mine through that coming winter until I let him loose again in the spring.

I often think of my trapping that flying squirrel and literally holding him in my hand. The creature was powerless. My hand determined its future. Hebrew thinking links the word "hand" (y'd) to the concept of power, and it often symbolizes power or strength. Someone's hand conveys authority involving responsibility, care, and dominion over someone or something. Hand is a recurring theme in 1 Samuel 23, occurring nine times in just 29 verses (verses 4, 6, 7, 11, 12, 14, 16, 17, and 20).[11] Seven times the usage of hand refers to a giving or handing over into someone's control—whether actually accomplished or not. The Philistines are given into David's hand (thus soundly defeated). Saul believes that God has delivered David into his hand. David wonders if the Keilahites will deliver him into Saul's hand. In verse 14 God does not deliver David into Saul's hand. Two verses later Jonathan strengthens David's hand in God. And in verse 6 Abiathar comes to David with an ephod in his hand. The hand is the terminal part of our arm used to perform the various functions of our will. Throughout the unfolding story of David's fugitive life hand symbolism represents power, strength, control, and trust (cf. Deut. 8:17; 1 Chron. 29:12; Isa. 59:1).

Scripture tells us the meaning of the deadly cat-and-mouse game that took place soon after David left Keilah. He decided that it would be safest for him to hide in the hill country of Ziph. To this rugged wilderness Saul and his troops came in pursuit of David. Every day they searched for him (1 Sam. 23:14). In this valley. Over that hill. From one cave to another. And every day, he successfully eluded capture. David, though, did not escape Saul because he was faster or more clever than Saul. No, he evaded the king because the Lord had intervened: "God did not deliver him into his hand" (verse 14, NASB). It is a daring theological interpretation.[12] The biblical author wants us to see the sovereign providence of God at work. Here Scripture contrasts the hand of a human being with the hand of God.

During this great chase the betraying Ziphites lead Saul to David (verses 19-28). The drama takes us hill by hill, cliff by cliff, crag by crag, rock by rock over the wilderness terrain of Maon until the king finally corners his prey. When David sees Saul and his army coming he is on a conical rock citadel atop a hill (verse 25). Suddenly, Saul has the rock nearly surrounded. A deadly battle pitting Israelite against Israelite seems inevitable, and yet David likely has the advantage and will win. After all, he is Israel's greatest military leader. Here he and his troops hold the physical high ground in the battlefield of their own choosing. But David chooses not to fight. He and his troops abandon their advantageous site and begin a militarily foolish but theologically wise retreat.[13] David flees down one side of the mountain while Saul charges up the opposite one, sending men at the same time around both flanks to encircle David and his forces. The king and his men are finally "closing in," ready to "capture." All seems lost for David. Saul almost has him in his grasp. Our imagination instinctively jumps ahead to the moment the king is sure to seize David. We wait. But just at the critical moment, Saul gets word that the Philistines have launched a massive invasion. They're wreaking havoc in the land. Abruptly he has no choice but to abort his near triumph. He is powerless to accomplish his greatest desire.

Consider the sequence of events that God had set in motion hours before and had injected into the situation. First, the Philistines had to decide that it was an opportune time to make a raid into Israel. While they came to this conclusion in their own minds, God was ruling and overruling to accomplish His will. Second, someone had to dispatch an Israelite runner to get help from the king, who was out in the field and likely on the move himself. Third, and the most critical of all, a narrow window of a few minutes surrounded the arrival time of the messenger. In just a few more minutes David would have been dead. On the other hand, if he had showed up too soon, David would not have seen the divine sovereign providence displayed on his behalf. The Lord brought the news of the Philistine invasion at just the right moment. God controls all things, as those who obey Him discover.[14]

God's precise timing delivers David. In recognition of this remarkable prevention of a bloody civil war and narrow escape,[15] the rock outcropping on which these events occurred came to be known as *Sela Hammahlekoth*—the "Rock of Escape." So many of those so-called coincidental moments in our lives have involved the hand of God. "The Lord's hand is not so short that it cannot save" (Isa. 59:1, NASB). Years later David would write: "in Your hand is power and might; and it lies in Your hand to make great and to strengthen everyone" (1 Chron. 29:12, NASB).

Hurting people hurt people, but healed people heal people. They want to help others. When we are consumed with our own problems we don't have the spiritual or emotional resources to think about others. But, as with David, God is present to heal our hurts so we can heal those of others.

When we've unplugged enough from our problems and purposefully connect with God with the resolve to know His will and wait on Him until He speaks and leads, like David, we too will be able to discern God's will. He will speak to us in the WirelessZone.

And when in that WirelessZone we experience betrayal or find ourselves chased like an animal through some dismal wilderness, we can be sure that the Lord's hand is not so short that it cannot save.

God inspired David to write Psalm 54 after the Ziphites told Saul his whereabouts. We can only imagine the scene. He is dirty, sweaty, hungry, thirsty, exhausted, and no doubt discouraged. The king has attacked him, and others have let him down. At the climax of a bizarre and adrenaline-pumping chase—just when it looks as though he isn't going to survive—Saul suddenly calls off his pursuit and leaves. The turn of events must have been nerveracking. David records his feelings, those expressions we have preserved in the lyrics of Psalm 54. He begins the psalm with the words "Save me, O God, by Your name" (NKJV). He calls God his helper and his sustainer (verse 4). David seems to have as many names for God as he has needs! Why? Because God is everything to him! Even when betrayed, wrongly accused, and hunted by ruthless men, David cannot let go of God. Abruptly released from the wild chase, he is nevertheless still helpless, a fugitive on the run. While delivered, he still needs rescue. And yet he ends with a promise to God: "I will sacrifice a freewill offering to you; I will praise your name, O Lord, for it is good. For he has delivered me from all my troubles, and my eyes have looked in triumph on my foes" (verses 6, 7, NIV). Freewill offerings are to be in proportion to the blessings one had receives from God (Deut. 16:10). Counting our blessings when we are betrayed, wrongly accused, and hunted by ruthless pursuers is different than counting our blessings in the safety of Sabbath worship. David responds to his helpless state by giving a freewill offering to God in proportion to His blessings.[16] In doing so, he leaves us a wonderful example of spiritual vitality and passion for God.

---

[1] Keith Kaynor, *When God Chooses: The Life of David*, p. 95.

[2] Alan Redpath, *The Making of a Man of God*, p. 88.

[3] Theodore Epp, *A Man After the Heart of God*, p. 60; Kaynor, p. 96.

[4] Beth Moore, *A Heart Like His: Intimate Reflections on the Life of David* (Nashville: Broadman and Holman Publishers, 1999), p. 92.

[5] Epp, p. 63.

[6] Walter Brueggemann, *First and Second Samuel*, p. 163.

[7] F. B. Meyer, *The Life of David*, p. 82.

[8] Kaynor, p. 97.

[9] Epp, pp. 61, 62.

[10] *Ibid.*, p. 65.

[11] See discussion by Peter D. Miscall, *1 Samuel: A Literary Reading* (Bloomington, Ind.: Indiana University Press, 1986), pp. 139, 140.

[12] Brueggemann, p. 163.

[13] Robert D. Bergen, *1, 2 Samuel,* pp. 236, 237.

[14] Kaynor, p. 100.

[15] Bergen, p. 237.

[16] Moore, p. 94.

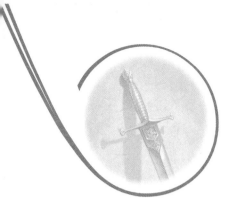

6

# LIFE'S MOST SUBTLE TEMPTATION

## I Samuel 24:1-22

E n-gedi is a small oasis running up a rugged crag alongside the Dead Sea. The Dead Sea is the large lake of salt water at the southeastern corner of Israel, some 1,300 feet below sea level. Today the oasis has a park for picnickers and swimmers—a cluster of palm trees, a restaurant where you can buy soft drinks and food, and bathhouses for changing and rinsing off the salt after a swim. You can't really swim in the dense salt water. You just float or bob around, hoping you don't accidentally swallow any of the terrible stuff—the water is extremely bitter and toxic. Since En-gedi is a favorite tourist stop, you will usually encounter a dozen or so such floaters and scores of people sunning themselves along the beach.

About 300 yards to the west of the picnic area you will see precipitous cliffs pushing up 2,000 feet and topped by a barren plateau. Erosion has deeply grooved the limestone plateau and cliffs, making a tangle of canyons and caves. It is a vast expanse of badlands, country as harsh and inhospitable as any you are likely to find anywhere on earth. And it is a place of breathless heat and scorching sun. Without head covering and water you soon wither from heat exhaustion. En-gedi is one of the few oases in this seemingly endless desert wilderness. The gully it follows up the cliffs is full of freshwater springs, waterfalls, pools, lush vegetation, and countless caves. It hasn't changed much since the days of David. That includes the presence of the ibex goats with their long and twisted horns that inhabit the rocky ravine. The creatures are fascinating to see along the hillside as you begin your way up. Scripture refers to this wilderness oasis as the "Rocks of the Wild Goats" (1 Sam. 24:2, NKJV).

I've spent time at En-gedi. More than once I've climbed up through the craggy wilderness to those cool waterfalls. I've waded in the pools and enjoyed the shade of the caves. Soaking in the musical sound of the water rushing over the falls, I've admired the dense thickets of tall grass and scrub brush, brush so thick you can't see through let alone make your way through. One can almost imagine an enemy or predatory animal lurking somewhere in there, ready to pounce—whether from the dense under-brush or the dark recesses of a cave. It is not hard imagining, either, the kind of life David eked out in that harsh environment. En-gedi was a per-fect place to hide, but nevertheless rugged. After his close call in the wilderness of Ziph, David and his men took refuge among the rocks and caves there (1 Sam. 23:29). The site provided protection and water and afforded a natural lookout spot from which they could see for miles around. There they could easily guard against any enemy's approach. The caves that pockmarked the cliffs were ideal places to camouflage their presence. Also En-gedi provided the advantage of high ground in the event of battle.

So there was David, safe and secure, with a bountiful supply of water in what Scripture calls "the strongholds of Engedi" (verse 29, NIV). As usual, someone had reported his whereabouts to Saul. So when the king finished averting the Philistine invasion that had pulled him away at the last minute from catching David at Ziph, he returned to the chase (verses 27, 28). Saul set out after David with 3,000 handpicked men. It's a rivet-ing fugitive drama: "After Saul returned from fighting the Philistines, he was told that David had gone into the wilderness of En-gedi. So Saul chose three thousand special troops from throughout Israel and went to search for David and his men near the rocks of the wild goats. At the place where the road passes some sheepfolds, Saul went into a cave to relieve himself. But as it happened, David and his men were hiding in that very cave! 'Now's your opportunity!' David's men whispered to him. 'Today is the day the Lord was talking about when he said, "I will certainly put Saul into your power, to do with as you wish."' Then David crept forward and cut off a piece of Saul's robe. But then David's conscience began bothering him because he had cut Saul's robe. 'The Lord knows I shouldn't have done it,' he said to his men. 'It is a serious thing to attack the Lord's anointed one, for the Lord himself has chosen him.' So David sharply rebuked his men and did not let them kill Saul" (1 Sam. 24:1-7, NLT).

Surely David had lookouts posted, so the king's presence in the En-gedi area did not take him by surprise. As Saul approached, David weighed the situation: should he run or hide? He decided to hide. But his blood must have frozen in his veins when Saul's columns halted outside the very cave in which he was hiding. Saul walked into the darkness of the cave. Temporarily blinded by the dark, he had no idea that David and his men were there. It must have been one of those days of breathless heat. Saul decided he needed to rest and entered the cave for the benefit of its quietness and coolness. He also had to go—literally! Evidently he turned around, dropped his drawers, and answered the call of nature.[1] Can you imagine the scene of numerous pairs of eyes glued on the king's backside? Talk about being vulnerable, about an embarrassing moment! Bad enough for the king to be seen at that moment, but to be in the very presence of the enemy. It is possible that Saul also lay down for a few moments to rest and drifted off to sleep. Scripture doesn't say for sure.

## Subtle Temptations

The king's vulnerability during this private moment was extreme, and David's soldiers knew it. In fact, the situation was so extraordinary that they concluded that God had made it happen to fulfill some prophecy of deliverance. Here, like Saul, they were quick to interpret circumstances as divine opportunity. The seconds must have seemed like centuries, the minutes like millennia. Then someone whispered, "It's the Lord's will to kill him! Go for it, man. Cut him down! He won't know what hit him."

It doesn't take a strong imagination to picture how they must have argued and pleaded with their leader to get rid of his enemy once and for all. It would mean an end to their hardship and suffering. And in the process David would become king, replacing an inept leader who had lost his credibility among the people. The land of Israel could be freed of its apostasy, idolatry, and threats from enemies. One simple act—for which he would be commended by most of his followers—would place wealth, power, and fame within his reach. And a poor king would get sacked. Wouldn't it be the best thing for God's people? Like many in our day, David's men very probably believed that the end justified the means, that opportunity provides its own moral justification.

Suddenly David had to confront a difficult choice as he faced three of life's most subtle temptations. He was tempted to get even with someone who had repeatedly wronged him and was making his life so painful (verse 12). But getting even with someone who has harmed us is not God's will for His people. The individual who walks in fellowship with Him will not seek personal revenge. But handling mistreatment does not come easy. It takes patience, self-restraint, a spirit of forgiveness, and love. Spiritual passion needs to be strong.

David also had to resist the temptation to read God's will into the circumstances unfolding before his very eyes.[2] Such a moment seems like a classic "the Lord's will" incentive. When we really want to support our idea, we say, "The Lord led me to do that." Or "The Lord has opened the door . . . or closed the door." The reality is that the Lord gets blamed for all sorts of things He has nothing to do with.[3] Opportunity itself does not provide moral justification. Higher values must govern our responses. We must always remember that in the heat of the moment we are the most vulnerable. Faith on the run can sometimes misread events and situations. Circumstances aren't always the clue to where God is leading or working. David's men jumped to the conclusion that God had set up the opportunity for him to take Saul's life. As Epp cautions: "We need to be exceedingly cautious how we interpret what we call God's providences, drawing our own conclusions from them rather than waiting to see God's purposes back of them."[4]

Furthermore, David had to resist the temptation to look upon and treat someone in authority disrespectfully. As Peterson observes: "All the ingredients for a scene of coarse vulgarity are here: the king on his 'throne,' viewed from the backside, taking a dump."[5] I can hear the snickers. The mockery. The contempt and disrespect. After all, Saul was an inept, flawed, and moody leader who had long ago lost credibility and respect with people. His relentless and unsuccessful search for David made him look stupid. Everyone knew what was going on. Everyone but his cronies wanted him gone. The prevailing mood was one of disrespect and undermining of authority. So why not poke fun behind his back? Why not lead the charge and get rid of him? Why not drop him in his own mess? It would be something to talk about and gloat over for a long long time.

### Conscience

So what did David do? He "arose and cut off the edge of Saul's robe secretly" (verse 4, NASB). Can't you see him? Saul's on his haunches, taking care of his business, looking out of the cave, and David sneaks up behind him and—*snip*—ever so silently cuts off a piece of the king's robe![6] Perhaps Saul had thrown his robe off to the side somewhere near where David was hiding, so it wasn't all that hard to do. Once he had done it, however, David became troubled. Scripture tells us his "conscience bothered him" (verse 5, NASB). Remorse and guilt filled him. Why? we may ask. He could have killed Saul, but he didn't. All he did was cut off part of the king's robe. What's the big deal? So his hem wasn't level anymore. Who's going to notice?

First, something going on in David's heart—something about his motives—troubled him deeply about what appears to be a harmless act. Had he actually contemplated killing Saul? Had he crept up behind Saul planning to kill him and at the very last moment decided only to slice off the corner of his garment? Or was his heart simply filled with pride, choosing a symbolic way to demonstrate to his men that he eventually would be the king of Israel? Perhaps he was going to taunt Saul in some way. Whatever his motives, David felt guilt-stricken.

A tender conscience is a good thing when God controls it. A conscience sensitized by God is a mark of spirituality. The stuff of spiritual passion, a conscience in tune with God's Word is a great asset. Our conscience is a vital part of our total being.[7] And our passion for God grows when we honor conscience. But nothing challenges spiritual passion more than when we go against that inner voice. God uses our conscience as a testing ground for conviction. Such conviction always probes our passion for Him. David nurtured a conscience that was in touch with the holiness of God—with God Himself. His passion for God ever called for that kind of careful inner listening.

One measurement of our passion for God is the length of time between conviction and repentance. Conviction must always result in a change of attitude or behavior. The Holy Spirit always does His job, but we don't always do ours! David responded to his Spirit-stricken conscience with an immediate change of behavior.[8] Expressing grief, he humbled himself before God and tuned himself to the holy. David was intimate with God at this point in his life.

Second, we must consider the symbolic nature of cutting off a corner of Saul's robe. Some suggest that the act was far from meaningless because David's confiscation of a portion of the royal robe signified the transfer of power from the house of Saul to the house of David. Furthermore, by removing the corner of the robe, David made Saul's robe to be in a state of noncompliance with Torah requirements (cf. Num. 15:38, 39; Deut. 22:12). Thus Saul's most obvious symbol of kingship became unwearable. In essence, David had symbolically invalidated the king's claim to rulership.[9]

Evidently David immediately recognized the powerful implications of his deed and felt conscience-stricken. He realized the nature of the indignity that he had imposed on a king. By voiding Saul's claim to kingship, he was essentially lifting his hand against "the Lord's anointed."[10] So he said to his men, "Far be it from me because of the Lord that I should do this thing to my lord, the Lord's anointed, to stretch out my hand against him, since he is the Lord's anointed" (1 Sam. 24:6, NASB). In David's mind, this was more than an act against the king. It was rebellion against the Lord, who had commanded His people not to curse their leaders (Ex. 22:28) or rebel and grumble against constituted authority (Num. 12:2-15; 16:1-35).[11] We tend to measure such moments in relative terms. David's standard for measuring them, however, was not the wickedness of Saul, but the holiness of God.[12]

Had Saul been wrong in his pursuit of David? Beyond the shadow of a doubt. Was the king a poor leader? Unquestionably. Did Saul have the genuine respect of his people? Absolutely not. Was it David's responsibility to make it right? No. That was God's job, in His way and in His own time. David realized that now. He saw that even in his little tantalizing mockery he had overstepped his bounds. "That's not right," he says. "There's a righteous principle here that I am breaking."

Ultimately David respected God more than he desired revenge. He withdrew from taking the life of Saul—or even undermining the king's honor and leadership—out of respect for God, not the king. If you are willing to honor a person out of reverence for God, you can be assured that God will honor you.[13] Your spiritual passion will deepen. When you respect a person out of honor to God, your own passion for God's honor will intensify. At the same time, God will restore or deepen your esteem for the person you have come to resent or are tempted to dishonor. God is always faithful! And passion for God is always the bottom line.

One of the most important lessons we can learn from this story concerns the proper way to respond to undeserving human authority. How do we change that authority without forfeiting God's blessing and in a way that we can preserve such authority for the benefit of future generations?[14] What do you do when a leader goes astray, or is incompetent, or has lost credibility? How can you maintain authority while replacing the person who holds it?

Sometimes social pressure muddies the waters and makes following conscience in matters of respecting leadership and authority difficult. Scripture tells us that "David persuaded his men with these words and did not allow them to rise up against Saul" (1 Sam. 24:7, NASB). Those around David encouraged him to vindicate himself by taking the corrupt king's life. How easy it would have been for him to accept their advice. But David persuaded them not to harm Saul. In other words, not only did he do the right thing, he brought the whole group with him. He stood strong against the tide of opinion. I have a feeling it wasn't easy. No doubt they went back and forth, back and forth, but David stood for a righteous principle until he at last convinced them.[15] The whispered dialogue must have been heated.

"Don't be a fool, David!"

"Hey, this wasn't right!"

"David, the guy's done everything but take your life. He's an inept no-good leader who's taking the country down with him. A real bumbling, moody jerk!"

"Look, I can't do it, and I can't let you do it either. He's the Lord's anointed. It's wrong!"

Social pressures can lead to devastating decisions, but David held fast to his convictions.[16] How easy it would have been for him to follow their advice! Sometimes around the water cooler, behind closed doors, in the hallway—wherever—we work each other up with attitudes of disrespect for leadership or retaliation against some wrong done.

I wonder about the difference there would be in our homes and in the workplace, at church and in the world, if our attitude toward leadership and authority were more reverent, more respectful, more supportive, more understanding. Maybe some of our children would still be in the church or at least would show us more respect. Perhaps our faith would be stronger. Or God's work would move forward more aggressively, and the blessing of God's Holy Spirit would come down upon us in richer, fuller measure. As a result, our witness to the world would be stronger, and we would see more baptisms. Above all, we would have more respect and awe and wonder and reverence for God. More passion for God!

I tell my sons that when I teach them to respect and honor me, their teachers, or other persons in authority in their/our world, I am helping them learn what it means to open their heart and yield to God. How can we have passion for God when our passion is one of disrespect? It is impossible.

### Waiting . . .

A most remarkable confrontation occurred in this moment of vulnerability for Saul and David. The king finished his business in the cave and went outside, completely oblivious to what had just happened. As he perhaps started down a ravine on the other side, David chugged out of the cave, clutching a piece of the royal robe in his hand. Saul was within earshot. David called out to the king across the chasm. It was a perilous moment because it betrayed the location of David and his men. Perhaps Saul himself would still have been vulnerable as well. What took place next are the longest recorded quotes by both David (114 Hebrew words) and Saul (67 Hebrew words), found in 1 Samuel.[17] The amount of space devoted to both quotations suggests their importance.

"David came out and shouted after him, 'My lord the king!'

"And when Saul looked around, David bowed low before him.

"Then he shouted to Saul, 'Why do you listen to the people who say I am trying to harm you? This very day you can see with your own eyes it isn't true. For the Lord placed you at my mercy back there in the cave, and some of my men told me to kill you, but I spared you. For I said, "I will never harm him—he is the Lord's anointed one." Look, my father, at what I have in my hand. It is a piece of your robe! I cut it off, but I didn't kill you. This proves that I am not trying to harm you and that I have not sinned against you, even though you have been hunting for me to kill me. The Lord will decide between us. Perhaps the Lord will punish you for what you are trying to do to me, but I will never harm you. As that old proverb says: "From evil people come evil deeds." So you can be sure I will never harm you. Who is the king of Israel trying to catch, anyway? Should he spend his time chasing one who is as worthless as a dead dog or a flea? May the Lord judge which of us is right and punish the guilty one. He is my advocate, and he will rescue me from your power!'

"Saul called back, 'Is that really you, my son David?'

"Then he began to cry. And he said to David, 'You are a better man than I am, for you have repaid me good for evil. Yes, you have been wonderfully kind to me today, for when the Lord put me in a place where you could have killed me, you didn't do it. Who else would let his enemy get away when he had him in his power? May the Lord reward you well for the kindness you have shown me today. And now I realize that you are surely going to be king, and Israel will flourish under your rule. Now, swear to me by the Lord that when that happens you will not kill my family and destroy my line of descendants!'

"So David promised, and Saul went home. But David and his men went back to their stronghold" (verses 8-22, NLT) .

It was a dramatic moment. Rather than cursing his ruler, David honored him by calling him both "my lord" and "the king." Rather than falling upon Saul in a murderous attack, David fell upon the ground "and prostrated himself with his face to the ground" (verse 8, NIV). Talk about passion for God!

Following these verbal and actional signals of loyalty to the king, David uttered what is perhaps the most passionate and eloquent plea for reconciliation between persons recorded in Scripture. In his appeal David tactfully avoided accusing Saul of being the one who initiated hurtful actions against him. It was not Saul but unnamed "men" (verse 9) who were lying to Saul about David, saying, "Behold, David seeks to harm you." "That's not true," he said. "And I can prove it!" Then David offered evidence of his good intentions toward Saul. He held up the piece of cloth that he had just sliced from Saul's garment. It was a visible exhibition that he could just as easily have cut off Saul's head. More important, David declared his motive for sparing the king: it was because he respectfully recognized that Saul "is the Lord's anointed." David treated the king properly, not because of anything the king had done or might do, but because of what the Lord had done. David based his respect for human authority on his respect for divine authority.[18]

David's language rose to the level of poetry as he put the king's recent efforts to hunt him down in perspective:

*After whom goes forth Israel's king?*
*After whom are you seeking?*
*After a lifeless dog?*
*A single flea?*

Thus David tacitly accused the king of acting like a fool and squandering precious national resources. Yet the rhetorical questions and the unflattering comparisons of himself as a dead dog and a flea—all expressed in a poetic framework—helped make David's criticisms more palatable and poignant.[19]

It worked! Saul's response was incredible. As Proverbs declares, "When a man's ways are pleasing to the Lord, he makes even his enemies to live at peace with him" (Prov. 16:7, NIV).

David was above all reverent.[20] When he looked at Saul, he did not see an enemy. Rather, he beheld the magnificent, albeit flawed, king chosen by God Himself and did obeisance. He turned that dark dusty cave that had become a latrine into a sacred place where he viewed God's glory where no one else could see it—in Saul.[21] Interestingly, by respecting authority now, David protected it for himself later. He preserved it too for future generations who would look back at his example. It was not just the 600 in the cave that he persuaded of his moral leadership. David won public approval and God's favor by not taking things into his own hands. He gained potentially unlimited future respect and national affection as a result of self-control now.[22]

David became a dynamic model to all of us who feel tempted to retaliate by hurting someone who has injured us—and who may be continuing to harm us. He is an example for all of us who must resist the temptation to read the circumstances around us through our own eyes rather than biblical principles. When we find ourselves tempted to undermine leadership or authority in any way or when we must resist the voices around us who would press us to compromise integrity and grumble and rebel against authority, David must be our role model.

Again, David's response forces us to deal with a few hard questions. His passion for God makes us wonder about ourselves. Think of a person in your life who has repeatedly tried to hurt you. Or a leader who for some reason has lost your respect or is just plain inept. Think about your attitudes and actions toward that individual. In your relationship with that person, is your conscience tuned to the will and Word of God, or to what you want to do to that person? Are you tempted to return evil for evil? Do you check your behavior before you do something irreversible and damaging to your personal testimony? Do you refuse to go along with the crowd in your attitudes and actions toward this unlovable person? When wronged and you need to defend yourself, do you do so with humility and respect? Do your attitudes and actions toward this person reflect that you believe God will ultimately make things right—even if you cannot? Does your passion for God enable you to treat that person with dignity and honor because you honor Him? How do you read unfolding circumstances in your life? Are you willing to wait and interpret them through biblical principles rather than the expediency of opportunity?

The kind of feelings and motives and attitudes lurking in my interior world are hard to get a handle on sometimes, let alone acknowledge or confess. But like David, I want to nurture a conscience that is in touch with the holiness of God—with God Himself. I desire that my passion for God should ever call for that kind of careful inner listening. My goal is always to tune my heart to the holy, toward reverence and humility, to God's Word and way.

> "How can I know all the sins lurking in my heart?
> Cleanse me from these hidden faults.
> Keep me from deliberate sins! Don't let them control me.
> Then I will be free of guilt and innocent of great sin.
> May the words of my mouth and the thoughts of my heart be
> pleasing to you, O Lord, my rock and my redeemer."
> —Psalm 19:12-14, NLT

"Teach me your way, O Lord,
    and I will walk in your truth;
give me an undivided heart,
    that I may fear your name.
I will praise you, O Lord my God,
    with all my heart; I will glorify your name forever.
For great is your love toward me."

—Psalm 86:11-13, NIV

---

[1] In the Hebrew, the phrase "went in to relieve himself" literally means "to cover his feet."

[2] Ellen G. White, *Patriarchs and Prophets,* p. 661.

[3] C. R. Swindoll, *David: A Man of Passion and Destiny,* p. 84.

[4] Theodore Epp, *A Man After the Heart of God,* p. 69.

[5] Eugene Peterson, *Leap Over a Wall,* p. 77.

[6] Swindoll, p. 85.

[7] Epp, p. 70.

[8] Beth Moore, *A Heart Like His,* p. 98.

[9] Robert D. Bergen, *1, 2 Samuel,* p. 239.

[10] *Ibid.*

[11] *Ibid.*

[12] Moore, p. 98.

[13] *Ibid.,* p. 99.

[14] Keith Kaynor, *When God Chooses: The Life of David,* p. 101.

[15] Swindoll, p. 86.

[16] Gene A. Getz, *David: Seeking God Faithfully,* p. 121.

[17] Bergen, p. 239.

[18] *Ibid.,* p. 240.

[19] *Ibid.,* p. 241.

[20] Peterson, p. 77.

[21] *Ibid.*

[22] Kaynor, p. 103.

7

# WHAT TO FEED AN ANGRY MAN

## I Samuel 25:1-42

Once upon a time a young couple climbed a high mountain. When they reached the top they came across a wise old man. Upon seeing them, he motioned for them to sit down. He told them they could ask him any question. So they inquired about the meaning of life, and he explained it. Next they asked him the recipe for happiness. The wise man wrote it down. The secrets of the universe? No problem. Then they brought up a *hard* question: "Oh, Great Master, we are angry so often. We hurt each other when we get angry. What can we do?" Suddenly the wise man glared at them, broke his pencil in two, cursed loudly, and stomped back into his cave. "Alas," he muttered over his shoulder, "if I could figure that out, I wouldn't be sitting here all alone on this mountain!"

Anger causes a lot of trouble in our lives. It is one of the most debilitating and paralyzing emotions we wrestle with. One reason anger is so destructive is that it is so unpredictable. And so painful. We hurt people when we get angry. And we feel our pain deep down inside when we've unleashed our anger. It can come almost before we know it and wear so many faces. Our lives can become a mess because of our anger. We can become enraged over the most ridiculous things. In the process we may say things we later regret, and then turn around and say them again. Because of anger we can destroy property, lose friends or our job, or make everybody around us walk on tiptoe. Guilt and shame and low self-esteem overwhelm us. It can make us perpetually cynical and hostile, uncooperative, aggressive. By generating interpersonal conflict in the home or workplace, anger ruins our health and emotional well-being. All this because of things we have done or the people we have hurt when we've been angry.

Anger has unbelievable power to threaten spiritual passion. As anger gains mastery of our heart it usurps our passion for God. It's a subtle force that overwhelms our sense of being.

Experts have outlined what they call the "anger and violence ladder."[1] The first rung is "sneaky anger." Sneaky anger simply seeks to frustrate somebody by purposely forgetting something, playing dumb, leaving things out, or just whining. We call that passive aggressive behavior in our home (getting back at people indirectly, without telling them why, rather than confronting them head-on)! Next comes the cold shoulder, followed by blaming and shaming, then swearing, screaming, and yelling. Demands and threats, chasing and holding—each forms ugly rungs on the way up. Partly controlled violence is the stage just before you reach the top—blind rage. The goal of partly controlled violence is power and control. One unleashes partly controlled violence in order to make others do what one wants, to show them who's boss. We attack on purpose and will stop only when we get our own way. The goal of blind rage is to destroy. At this level we are usually out of control. Kill or be killed. That is why blind rage is so dangerous.

When Nabal refused to provide food for David's hungry men, their leader's blood ran so hot that he instantly hit the anger and violence ladder's top rung—blind rage! The story unfolds like several scenes in a one-act play. Before we get too far into the plot, though, let's get some background.

First Samuel 25 opens with a most significant event: the death of Samuel. "Now Samuel died; and all Israel assembled and mourned for him. They buried him at his home in Ramah. Then David got up and went down to the wilderness of Paran" (1 Sam. 25:1, NRSV). Samuel had been Israel's spiritual conscience, spokesperson for God, and anointer of kings. He had anointed Saul and watched him turn away from God and fail. Then he anointed David, witnessed him succeed at first, then run for his life. The prophet never saw this young man after God's own heart ascend Israel's throne. Under the worst of circumstances, Samuel was the best of men. He was a rare gem, faithful to God to the end. I cannot express how much I want that kind of longstanding passion for God—to be faithful as was Samuel to my very last breath!

This chapter in David's life, then, opens with tremendous loss. Samuel had been David's mentor. He was the lone spiritual link affirming his anointing as Israel's next king—that he would make it, that God's will would prevail. That Saul would not succeed in killing him. Significantly, this chapter also concludes with the mention of another loss. Saul had given David's wife Michal to another man (verse 44). It was something that David took very personally. Years later he would demand her back (2 Sam. 3:13, 14). One senses that his desire to get her back was more than just a matter of male honor. Her husband at the time cried his heart out and followed the woman for miles when Abner came and took her away as part of a deal he had worked out with David (verses 15, 16). Would David have felt any different when she was taken away from him? She was the bride of his youth for whom he had risked his life to bring Philistine foreskins as dowry.

Overwhelmed and surrounded by pain, he must have wondered if God would ever avenge Saul's evil and uphold his integrity. Tired and sad, David left the cool of En-gedi to scratch out some sort of living in the wilderness of Paran. There he and his men found themselves living in the same area where Nabal's shepherds grazed his sheep. In fact, David and his army had often protected Nabal's shepherds and their animals from harm and danger. David was responsible for the welfare of 600 men. He needed food for their hungry stomachs and clothes for their backs. No doubt he anticipated that if he helped the shepherds, their master, Nabal, would reciprocate. It was customary for landowners such as Nabal to compensate their protectors with a small portion of the harvest and the herds.

### When Men Are Hungry

In order to further understand David's frame of mind, skip dinner—for a couple of days. How about for several weeks! The problem of supplying 600 men with food seems to have been the catalyst for explosion. Men do strange things when deprived of adequate provisions.[2] When men are hungry, they can become more than a little testy. Add to that the high-adrenaline life of a fugitive living in the rugged wilderness.

It all started when Nabal was cashing in on his investments. It was sheepshearing season. Time to collect the wool and the profits from his vast enterprise. For most people this was an opportunity to share material blessings with others. Knowing this, David sent 10 of his men to talk with Nabal about the need for food and clothing to take care of his army. After all, they had treated the landowner well, helping guard his flocks and protecting his shepherds. David's request was logical and reasonable. His men greeted Nabal appropriately and simply appealed to the custom of the day. But the wealthy Nabal was a surly and mean man. To David's surprise, the irritable landowner insulted him, treated his men discourteously, and sent them away empty-handed (1 Sam. 25:10-12).

The reader first encounters Nabal in terms of his possessions (verse 2). In other words, his possessions precede his own person. A wealthy landowner near the village of Carmel, he has 3,000 sheep and 1,000 goats. His property determines his life. He lives to defend his property, and he dies enjoying his property. Only after the narrator tells us of his riches do we learn the man's name.[3] His name says it all: he is a *fool*—the Hebrew word *nabal*. Caring only for himself, he is harsh and evil in his dealings (verse 3). Unlike Nabal, his wife, Abigail, is intelligent—clear-thinking and wise. Just the opposite of her husband, she is generous, kind, and lovely.

The provocation of Nabal seems almost deliberate on David's part. On the surface, his initial instruction to his men appears like an act of masterful intimidation (verses 5-8). David sends word to the landowner during the festival at the time of sheepshearing. He approaches the man when his wealth is especially available, visible, and hence vulnerable. While David's men begin with conventional words of greeting—"Have a long life, peace be to you, and peace be to your house, and peace be to all that you have" (verse 6, NASB)—one could interpret it as a message of intimidation and confiscation. A warning that Nabal's peace may be in jeopardy. David's men remind him that their leader has done no harm to the landowner's flock: "You are shearing your sheep and goats. While your shepherds stayed among us near Carmel, we never harmed them, and nothing was ever stolen from them. Ask your own servants, and they will tell you this is true. So would you please be kind to us, since we have come at a time of celebration? Please give us any provisions you might have on hand" (verses 7, 8, NLT). We could read that very reminder as an implicit threat that David might do harm now or withdraw his protection. Was this a subtle but unmistakable request for protection money? A Mafia-style extortion?[4] After all, David's men were a motley crew of malcontents (1 Sam. 22:2).

In reality, David was a good Samaritan. The herders who cared for Nabal's flocks were especially vulnerable to wilderness outlaws and rustlers. For at least one season David had provided protection. Nabal's herders testified to the fact that David was no extortioner. Later in the story one of Nabal's shepherds paints a glowing word picture of David's person and presence: "David's men were very good to us, and we never suffered any harm from them. Nothing was stolen from us the whole time they were with us. In fact, day and night they were like a wall of protection to us and the sheep" (1 Sam. 25:15, 16, NLT).

"'Who is this fellow David?' Nabal sneered. 'Who does this son of Jesse think he is? There are lots of servants these days who run away from their masters. Should I take my bread and water and the meat I've slaughtered for my shearers and give it to a band of outlaws who come from who knows where?'" (verses 10, 11, NLT). Clearly Nabal knew who David was, yet he pretended ignorance, making him out to be a nobody. Attempting to discredit David, he accuses him of being a rebellious runaway. He tries to justify his actions by inferring that David's men are rebels, outlaws who do not care to be tied down to the responsibilities of home or government. "Hey, I'm in big business. I do not deal with beggars, marauders, gypsies, or tramps. Nor do I pay protection money. There's no real threat against my business. If there is, I can handle it on my own. I don't need the likes of David and his bunch of losers."[5]

David was totally unprepared for Nabal's reaction. The landowner hurled the greatest insult at him that any man could ever give another. It was an offense that David took personally, devastating his ego. It hit him at one of the basic levels where anger so often erupts—self-esteem. In David's case, it was as if someone had tossed a match onto a pile of dry hay. In a moment he was aflame with revenge.

For years David had modeled patience under the spear of Saul. Patience with people betraying him and with the stresses of fugitive life.

But now he lost control. Literally insane with anger, he grabbed his sword and ordered 400 other men to do the same. There and then he vowed he would kill every man associated with Nabal (verse 13). "A lot of good it did to help this fellow," David exclaimed. "We protected his flocks in the wilderness, and nothing he owned was lost or stolen. But he has repaid me evil for good. May God deal with me severely if even one man of his household is still alive tomorrow morning!" (verses 21, 22, NLT). Interestingly, the term *male* in the Hebrew has the explicit reference "those who [urinate] against the wall." Thus he categorizes the male members of Nabal's company by their method of urination. People in Scripture regularly employ the phrase for those whom they despise.[6] In his anger David used the p word!

Thus Nabal's vulgarity provoked a like vulgarity in David.[7] Nabal the fool had stripped David's spiritual passion to the core, propelling him down the fool's path. When he lost his temper, David lost all sense of his identity as God's anointed. He was on the verge of becoming another Saul, out to get rid of anyone threatening his status and role.

Blind rage was about to lead David to do something he would regret the rest of his life. If it were not for a woman named Abigail, he would have been guilty of murder.

### The Beautiful Intercessor

At this point in the story the author introduces us to Nabal's beautiful wife, Abigail. When the servants heard how uncouth her husband had been to David's men, they went to speak to her. The surly and mean stupidity of Nabal must have been common knowledge and accepted fact.[8]

Abigail is a complete contrast to Nabal. Unlike her husband, she was no fool. Just the opposite of him, she was kind and lovely. They vastly differed in temperament, attitude, and philosophy of life. Abigail was "an intelligent and beautiful woman" (verse 3, NIV). She was as beautiful inwardly as she was outwardly. The combination of intelligence and beauty makes Abigail an obvious counterpart to David himself. They are two of a kind. Interestingly, Scripture uses the same Hebrew word for "beautiful" to describe the physical appearance of both David (1 Sam. 16:12) and Abigail (1 Sam. 25:3). The author employs the same Hebrew word for "understanding" to describe their heart as well, i.e., *sakal,* the word meaning "to act wisely" or "to act with understanding" that we learned about earlier. Scripture repeatedly tells us that David "behaved himself wisely" in all his ways (1 Sam. 18:5, 14, 15, 30). So with Abigail. In both cases, it is the "heart" and the "understanding" that matter in the story. Nabal and Abigail exemplify respectively what the wisdom tradition means by "foolish" and "wise."[9] Embroiled in anger, David, who has been known for behaving wisely, now is about to act the fool.

Fortunately, Nabal's servants knew their mistress had more sense than Nabal. A servant reported what her husband had done. Explaining how David's men had protected them in the fields, he warned her of the approaching storm. "You'd better think fast," he said, "for there is going to be trouble for our master and his whole family. He's so ill-tempered that no one can even talk to him!" (1 Sam. 25:17, NLT). Quickly Abigail gathered a generous amount of food and wine—probably prepared for Nabal's sheepshearing banquet—and hurried to intercept David in the hills (verses 18-20). When she reached him, she fell at his feet, taking the blame for her husband's irresponsible actions. Begging for mercy, she minced no words in describing her worthless husband (verses 24, 25). And all the food! Lots of food from a beautiful woman; who could resist? In addition, Abigail poured the cool water of logic, personal charm, and confession on David's hot head. All with a view to calling him back to his better self.

"Please forgive me if I have offended in any way," she pleads. "The Lord will surely reward you with a lasting dynasty, for you are fighting the Lord's battles. And you have not done wrong throughout your entire life. Even when you are chased by those who seek your life, you are safe in the care of the Lord your God, secure in his treasure pouch! But the lives of your enemies will disappear like stones shot from a sling! When the Lord has done all he promised and has made you leader of Israel, don't let this be a blemish on your record. Then you won't have to carry on your conscience the staggering burden of needless bloodshed and vengeance. And when the Lord has done these great things for you, please remember me!" (verses 28-31, NLT).

Awesome words, don't you think? Abigail appealed to David to put things in perspective. Nabal is a fool and should not be taken seriously. In fact, her very presence has in fact effectively eliminated him. He has ceased to exist as a serious character in the story.[10] So don't take things personally, she urged. Then Abigail "made it plain to David that the unkind course of her husband was in no wise premeditated against him as a personal affront, but was simply the outburst of an unhappy and selfish nature."[11] "Nabal is a fool, but you don't have to become a fool," she implied. David lost his temper because a fool had rejected him. He became so angry that he almost murdered a number of innocent men—all because of wounded ego. How ironic! David's incredible patience toward Saul is almost beyond comprehension. He had plenty reason to lose his cool over the things Saul did, but not with Nabal. Nabal was a fool. In Ecclesiastes Solomon writes, "Do not be quickly provoked in your spirit, for anger resides in the lap of fools" (Eccl. 7:9, NIV). As we have noted already, David was in danger of becoming a fool himself.

Abigail also sought to get David to view the bigger picture. "Look at what God has in mind for you," she said. "Look at who you are! As I behold you, I'm seeing the next king. A great king like David does not need to bear the mark of petty vengeance. Don't ruin your record with a murder. You're bigger than that, David. You have been wronged, but murder isn't the answer. Wait, David. Take what I've provided and turn around and go back. If you are fighting the Lord's battles there is no room for self or for doing evil. You'll have to live with a track record, David. You don't need this! Remember who you are. Don't forget God's anointing, God's mercy. And don't stoop to fighting grudge battles. Your task is to fight the battles of the Lord."[12] Great advice, don't you think?

Finally, Abigail concluded with the statement "And when the Lord has done these great things for you, please remember me!" (1 Sam. 25:31, NLT). "Remember me when you come to your throne. Remember me in gratitude. Remember me as the one who talked sense to you. Remember me as the one who protected your coming regime from the blood of Nabal. Remember me for my own well-being, for unless you remember me, I am left only with this hopeless Nabal."[13] Obviously we have here the personal dimension of a woman stuck in an unhappy situation. But there is also the reality that in the blessings and privileges David will experience because of his restraint now, he will look back and say that wisdom in the heat of passion is always the best route.

Abigail seemed to understand everything. Many a wife has to put up with this kind of husband, this kind of conflict management, in both the home and community. Praise God for women of intelligence!

## Restraining Grace

Remarkably, David stopped, looked, and listened. Abigail, this beautiful woman in the middle of nowhere, food in her hand and supplicating David on her knees, managed to bring God back into his life through humble yet carefully chosen and wise words. David let her speak. Suddenly the accelerating momentum of the story pauses and then reverses. Just as quickly as David lost control of his emotions, he regained perspective. He saw what he was about to do. The humble woman's openness and honesty touched his heart.

How can any hungry man remain mad when a beautiful woman shows up with a potful of delicious food? It's hard not to listen to what she has to say. Abigail's beauty surprised David. Through it he both sees and hears God again.[14] As Peterson writes: "In the presence of the beautiful we intuitively respond in delight, wanting to be involved, getting near, entering in—tapping our feet, humming along, touching, kissing, meditating, contemplating, imitating, believing, praying. Painted prayers; sung prayers; danced prayers. It's the very nature of our five senses to pull us into whatever is there—scent, rhythm, texture, vision."[15] "Beauty releases light into our awareness so that we're conscious of the beauty of the Lord. . . . Abigail's beauty puts David in touch, again, with the beauty of the Lord. He realizes who he is, what he's doing, what his life is for."[16]

God has given women a tremendous capacity to sway others. Their communication skills, their focus on deep relationships and care for others, and their physical attractiveness designed by God are all ways that women influence. God's first human creation was male, after which He said, "It is not good for the man to be alone. I will make a helper suitable for him" (Gen. 2:18, NIV). The Hebrew word for "helper" (*azer*) means "to surround." When women surround the men and women in their life with their relational skills and their care for others they become women of impact.[17] Abigail's effect on David is a biblical classic. He was all charged up with anger and out to take revenge for the ill treatment he had received from her husband. But along came Abigail with the right words said in the right way. And David went away, not saying, "Wow, what a woman!" but praising God. She recovered for him the identity that God had given him. It's an incredible image of communication skill, beauty, and sensitivity as she influences a man to honor God.

Through the actions of Abigail God wants us to see how He graciously works to keep us from sin and its scars—a great evidence of His mercy. Twice our passage makes this point: first from the lips of Abigail: "Now therefore, my lord, as the Lord lives, and as your soul lives, since the Lord has restrained you from shedding blood, and from avenging yourself by your own hand . . ." (1 Sam. 25:26, NASB); and second from David himself: "Blessed be the Lord God of Israel, who sent you this day to meet me, and blessed be your discernment, and blessed be you, who have kept me this day from bloodshed and from avenging myself by my own hand. Nevertheless, as the Lord God of Israel lives, who has restrained me from harming you, unless you had come quickly to meet me, surely there would not have been left to Nabal until the morning light as much as one male" (verses 32-34, NASB).

In short, God kept David from taking vengeance upon Nabal. Had his rage gone unchecked, he would have regretted it. But the Lord worked to negate his foolishness. After all, He had plans for David that would be altered significantly were the man to stoop to vengeance. It raises the question of what God has in mind for each one of us, and how any moral failure could unfit us for that vision.

With a humble heart David received the rebuke. He gave thanks and blessing because Abigail had advised him righteously. "Let the righteous smite me; it shall be a kindness: and let him reprove me; it shall be an excellent oil" (Ps. 141:5). As Ellen White writes, "how few take reproof with gratitude of heart and bless those who seek to save them from pursuing an evil course."[18] We thus catch another glimpse of David's heart. He is capable of violence. Yet here he does not harbor grudges or hang on to resentments. And he is teachable. May God forever keep us flexible and teachable.

There emerges here a picture of God as one who is interested in us as individuals and as one who may come to us through another person whom He has sent to us to save us from a sinful deed.[19] In times of decision and wrath, God has come to many a man through the quiet voice of his wife as she urged him to restraint and insisted that he leave vengeance to God.[20]

We learn too from this incident how comparatively small things may suddenly overwhelm and defeat us, even though we might have handled greater trials victoriously.[21] So far we have observed quite a mix of things in David's life—loss of a mentor, his wife, and his self-respect; the emotional roller-coaster ride of fugitive living with all its twists and turns; and the emotional effects of hunger. All exhausting and passion-draining. When faith is on the run, comparatively small things can set off an unexpected explosion.

I remember the time I trashed a $1,000 laser printer. It had been acting up for weeks. Paper would jam at the most inopportune moment—usually when I was in a hurry to meet a deadline. I would clear it, only to have it jam again. Even though I would take the covers off, wipe the rollers, and clean the grippers, it would still jam.

My real frustration, though, was not the machine. Painful developments, of which I had no control whatsoever, had been taking place in my staff and congregation. For weeks a friend's pain had been unraveling to my deep sorrow and utter helplessness. It was an emotionally exhausting time, demanding resources and wisdom beyond my power.

I was working on one of those never-ending deadlines when my printer jammed. I cleared it. Again it jammed. Taking the cover off, I cleaned the rollers. The printer jammed, fed a sheet, and jammed again. It was a frustrating cycle. Clear and jam. Clean and jam. Clear and jam. Jam! Jam! Jam! Then I picked the block of frustration off the credenza and threw it on the floor. Just like that. A thousand dollars. I could have salvaged it even then. But I kicked it. Twice. A few pieces fell off. Picking it up, I threw it around the room a few more times. A few more kicks. Then I sat down and cried.

I wasn't even thinking of the printer or the $1,000. I was overwhelmed with pain for my friends, my own helplessness, and the reality that I had come to a breaking point. The emotional roller-coaster ride of the past few weeks had depleted my spiritual passion. In the confusing maze of real life, anger rose up like a monster. Fortunately it was only a printer that got trashed. Not someone I loved or was responsible for. And not someone who needed my ministry during this stressful experience. It was a deeply humbling moment, filled with tears and quiet waiting on the Lord. He needed to renew me, needed to give me what I lost. I kept the control panel of the printer as a souvenir of that explosion of anger.

David's experience with Nabal and Abigail can help us come to grips with how we handle anger in our own heart and how we relate to it in others. Dealing with anger involves understanding self and self-control. Will we express anger outwardly, hold it in, or control and resolve it? Why am I angry? What sets me off? What is the source of other people's anger? What events have created frustration and anxiety—worn me or someone else down until we exploded? What is the straw that broke the camel's back? Do I have a quick temper? What can I do to keep from getting caught off guard? Sometimes people who are angry use others as scapegoats. Even though you may be the object of the attack, you may not be the primary source of frustration. Nor the person you are attacking!

Anger often relates significantly to our self-image—particularly a wounded ego. It is frequently easier to handle physical threats than psychological ones. Insecurity breeds quick tempers. And so does the loss of something important to us. Never try to get even or take vengeance on someone who has hurt you. Don't counter anger with anger. And try to understand the source of anger in yourself or the other person. Let biblical principles determine your responses. "My dear brothers, take note of this: Everyone should be quick to listen, slow to speak and slow to become angry, for man's anger does not bring about the righteous life that God desires" (James 1:19, 20, NIV). "Do not be quickly provoked in your spirit, for anger resides in the lap of fools" (Eccl. 7:9, NIV). "'In your anger do not sin': Do not let the sun go down while you are still angry, and do not give the devil a foothold" (Eph. 4:26, NIV).

Anger has unbelievable power to threaten spiritual passion. As anger gains mastery of our heart it usurps our passion for God. It overwhelms one's sense of being. Only a humble heart before God keeps our passion focused on His honor.

One more intriguing detail rounds out this astonishing chapter in David's life. After he received Abigail's gift of food, he sent her on her way with a blessing of shalom (peace). Abigail returned home after rescuing Nabal to find her drunken husband throwing a party. Imagine how she must have felt at that moment. Though tired and emotionally spent, she wisely let him sleep it off before telling him about her trip to see David. Apparently the news was too much for his blood pressure. He literally froze like a stone (became paralyzed) and died 10 days later.

But there's more! When David heard that Nabal was dead, he said, "Praise be to the Lord, who has upheld my cause against Nabal for treating me with contempt. He has kept his servant from doing wrong and has brought Nabal's wrongdoing down on his own head" (1 Sam. 25:39, NIV). Then David wasted no time in sending messengers to Abigail to ask her to become his wife. Not surprisingly, she accepted. It sounds like good romance and a happy ending for those who put their trust in God. But there's just one little problem. David went a bit overboard in the marriage department. We could understand about his shattered vows to Michal. After all, Saul had given his wife away to Paltiel (verse 44). But what about his marriage to Ahinoam, sandwiched there between his marriage to Abigail and his loss of Michal (verse 43)? When did he come up with her?

All of a sudden the narrative jerks us from celebrating Abigail's good fortune (and the romance of it all) to the fact that she had to share her man with another wife! We cannot help wondering. Did God tolerate David's actions? Did He make exceptions regarding marriage in the lives of kings? Did David's polygamy in any way affect his spiritual passion? Some things we may never understand, but one principle is definitely clear: polygamy has never been God's will (Gen. 2:24). Furthermore, Deuteronomy 17 contains regulations for the time when Israel would have kings. Kings were not to multiply wives lest it lead their hearts astray (verse 17). David knew that God intended him to be Israel's next king. Already he had disobeyed one of the Lord's specific commands for kings. We can take a moment to inhale deeply and smell trouble brewing. Eventually David's heart would get led astray. In our next volume we will, unfortunately, witness the tragedy caused by David's wandering heart. We will observe incredible inner pain, moral failure, and interpersonal conflict—definitely not the stuff of spiritual passion.[22]

---

[1] Ron Potter-Efron, *Angry All the Time: An Emergency Guide to Anger Control* (Oakland: New Harbinger Publications, Inc., 1994), pp. 49-60.
[2] Keith Kaynor, *When God Chooses: The Life of David*, p. 110.
[3] Walter Brueggemann, *First and Second Samuel*, p. 175.

[4] Brueggemann thinks so. See p. 176.

[5] See Brueggemann, pp. 176, 177.

[6] *Ibid.,* p. 178.

[7] Eugene Peterson, *Leap Over a Wall,* p. 83.

[8] Kaynor, p. 113.

[9] Brueggemann, p. 176.

[10] *Ibid.,* p. 178.

[11] Ellen G. White, *Patriarchs and Prophets,* p. 666.

[12] Peterson, p. 84.

[13] Brueggemann, p. 179.

[14] Peterson, p. 85.

[15] *Ibid.,* pp. 85, 86.

[16] *Ibid.,* p. 86.

[17] Vollie Sanders, "Biblical Femininity: What Does It Mean to Be a Woman?" *Discipleship* 77 (September/October 1993): 52-55.

[18] White, *Patriarchs and Prophets,* p. 667.

[19] Holmes Rolston, *Personalities Around David* (Richmond, Va.: John Knox Press, 1968), p. 102.

[20] *Ibid.*

[21] Kaynor, p. 116.

[22] I am indebted to Beth Moore for her insights into this seemingly insignificant detail of David's fugitive years (*A Heart Like His,* pp. 103, 104).

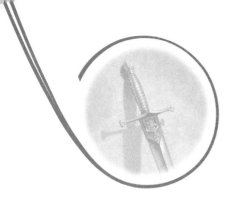

8

# WHERE EAGLES DARE AND TEMPTATION CALLS AGAIN

## I Samuel 26

While the Tet Offensive was exploding with full force in Vietnam, Hollywood released the World War II espionage thriller *Where Eagles Dare*. Richard Burton and Clint Eastwood costarred in this white-knuckle tale of an elite group of commandos on a mission to rescue an American general held captive by the Nazis in a castle high in the Bavarian Alps. Infiltrating the castle was difficult. The only way in was by cable-lift gondola. Security was tight. And not all the commandos were on the same side. A few years later I saw it when it appeared on TV. I was home from college one weekend and my dad asked me to watch it with him in the living room. All I can remember was that there were so many twists and turns in the story that it was impossible to predict the next scene. It left me sitting on the edge of my seat the whole way through. The suspense never ended until the surprise conclusion. I left exhausted and my mind stirred with images of high drama (with the advances in the movie industry, I can only imagine the adrenaline letdown after viewing some of our contemporary espionage thrillers).

While *Where Eagles Dare* had plenty of explosions and machine-gun fire near the end, now looking back, I remember it more of a saga of cool, calculated courage rather than glorification of war and violence. Burton and Eastwood were masters at that. They were daring-do guys with lots of guts. I've known a few guys in real life like that, including my father, who served in special forces in the South Pacific during World War II. One man shared so many incredible stories of his death-defying missions as a Night Raider assassin and saboteur on Japanese-occupied islands during World War II that I wondered how he ever made it back emotionally and psychologically, let alone with his life. I've always been intrigued by their stories and wonder how they did what they did. Could I handle that kind of stuff? I'm glad I've never needed to find out!

David's commando raid into Saul's sleeping camp is classic drama marked by cool calculated boldness and courage. It reveals something of a daredevil streak in him. What ordinary guy would invade the enemy's camp just to take a spear and water jug?[1]

For most of our story Saul has been the stalker seeking David. Now suddenly their roles reverse. Abruptly and unexpectedly, Saul is the hunted one and David the hunter.[2] By this time in the narrative David had moved back into the wilderness of Ziph, where it was easier for him and his men to find food and live. The Ziphites, though, betrayed him to Saul a second time. Saul marched without delay with a band of 3,000 young warriors to surprise his hated son-in-law at the hill of Hachilah, pointed out as the place of David's encampment (1 Sam 26:1-3).

When David received word of the expedition against him, he sent out spies to find out Saul's position. When they brought back to him the report that Saul lay encamped with his men at the foot of the hill of Hachilah, David took two of his men to check things out for himself (verses 4, 5). One of those daring reconnaissance operatives was Ahimelech the Hittite. Ahimelech was a descendant of one of the Canaanitish tribes who had converted to the faith of Israel. The other special-op was Abishai, the son of David's half sister Zeruiah. He was also the brother of Joab, who would later become David's military commander.

Creeping stealthily through the rocky defiles and thick undergrowth, the three commandos came so near to the royal camp that, from the elevation on which they lay, they could see everything. It was a hazardous venture, to say the least. Night had spread its dark veil over the rugged land. Deep silence reigned in the camp below. No doubt everyone was exhausted from the day's march through the rugged wilderness. Studying the scene, David realized that everyone in camp was already in a deep slumber. Saul slept quietly, his forces deployed around him. Having been on maneuvers with the king, David knew exactly where to look for him among the tents. In the pale moonlight they were able to make out the middle of the encampment where Saul and Abner, the commander of his army, now slept. It was a perfect setting for a favored military tactic—a predawn raid on a hostile camp.

Viewing the sleeping encampment below, David suddenly got a hare-brained idea. "Who will go down with me to Saul in the camp?" he whispered. It was a bold thought—nervy. So nervy that it startled Ahimelech, and he hesitated. He had to think that one over. The idea instantly energized Abishai, however. "I will go down with you," he exclaimed passionately. So the two commandos stealthily crept down from the rocky height into the valley. They slipped past the sleeping sentries and quietly made their way to the center of the encampment. There before them lay Saul, overpowered by sleep. His spear, the emblem of his sovereignty, was stuck in the ground at his bolster. By his side lay Abner, the man who ought to have kept watch over him while the king was asleep.

### The Terminator's Way

As they took in the scene together, Abishai whispered, "Today God has delivered your enemy into your hands" (verse 8, NIV). There they stood with Saul's spear within instant reach. How easy it would have been to plunge it into the rebellious king's heart! Once again David faced a choice: to kill or not to kill Saul. Temptations may vary from situation to situation, but they may also be very similar. In a previous chapter we saw David tested in a manner very much like what we read about here. Again he had the opportunity to take the life of Saul if he so desired. In some respects the circumstances are alike, and yet in others they differ. David needed more faith and more confidence in the Lord this second time than he did the first.[3]

The dissimilarities between the occasion David spared Saul's life in the cave (1 Sam. 24) and the encounter in Saul's sleeping camp are significant.[4] First, the two confrontations began in different ways. In the cave Saul came to where David was hiding. The opportunity was unplanned, unexpected, and immediate. David did not ask for it or arrange it, and it demanded an instant decision. There Saul was just as vulnerable as he could ever be. The camp situation, however, was David's choice.

Second, had David killed Saul in the cave, sooner or later the troops outside would have investigated and discovered David's presence. At the very least, everyone would have learned that David had taken vengeance on Saul. But here all were under a heavy sleep sent from the Lord, and no one would have known who had slain their leader.

Third, if David had taken Saul's life in the cave, the soldiers who waited outside could have then killed David. If enough of Saul's soldiers favored David, he might have lived, but his reputation would have suffered. If the king's killer went undetected in the camp, however, it would have seriously weakened the house of Saul. David would stand a good chance to become king while Saul's death would have greatly embarrassed Abner and perhaps put him under suspicion, since he was in a position to profit most from his ruler's death.

Of all the inducements to kill Saul, the most enticing was just the prospect itself. As Kaynor writes: "When unprincipled men are confronted with opportunity, they serve their own purposes. And the very existence of opportunity often nudges people into doing something they never intended to do. Opportunity! It makes up for any lack of logic and provides sufficient impetus for whatever is desired. Few have sufficient spiritual strength to resist. And of all opportunities, none are so strong and work so powerfully upon the will as those that seem to come from God."[5]

How strangely things can combine to make the wrong course of action appear right. We often call such situations "open doors." Because an opportunity presents itself, we assume it must be God's will to move forward. But determining God's will involves much more than merely assuming that every "open door" is an invitation from God. Moral and spiritual principles must guide our thinking. Only passion for God keeps opportunity from subverting the kind of thinking that spiritual integrity and wisdom demand.

Interpreting their remarkable success in penetrating the defenses as proof that God has delivered David's enemy into their hands, Abishai wants to be a good steward of the opportunity. "Give me the honor, sir," he whispers. "Please let me strike him with the spear to the ground with one stroke, and I will not strike him the second time" (1 Sam. 26:8, NASB).

I picture him as one of Hollywood's dramatic, muscular action heroes of choice—an Arnold Schwarzenegger or Steven Seagal. Abishai was one of the notorious sons of Zeruiah (David's half sister) who would make life so tumultuous once David became king.[6] The sons of Zeruiah were David's kinsmen and his most loyal and ruthless accomplices. Fearless, they were unquestioning in their devotion to David and always ready to kill.[7] Abishai was also a member of David's elite 30 (2 Sam. 23:8-39)—something we'll learn about in the next volume.

The bottom line is that Abishai was always ready to strike a crucial blow. In succeeding years he wanted to cut off Shimei's head (2 Sam. 16:5-11; cf. 19:22), killed Ishbi-benob, a Philistine champion, in order to save David during hand-to-hand combat (2 Sam. 21:16, 17), and participated in the assassination of Abner (2 Sam. 3:30). That's not all. He was involved in a lot of other bloody exploits with his brother Joab (2 Sam. 2:18-24; 10:9-14; 18:2-14; 20:6-10). The two brothers were so aggressive that David later complained about their violence (2 Sam. 3:39; 16:10; 19:23). Small wonder that Abishai was ready to sneak into Saul's camp or volunteered to do the killing himself. When he bragged that he could pin Saul to the ground with one thrust of the spear, he was fully capable of doing it, too.

Abishai reminds me of Vladimir Putin when he first became Russia's president. A no-nonsense former KGB man, Putin made it clear that he was comfortable with the use of force. "You have to hit first," he stated, "and hit so hard that your opponent will not get to his feet."[8] It's a philosophy that he sought to live up to in Chechnya.

Standing over Saul, David had to make a choice. Would it be the way of Abishai? Or that of God? Should he seek a good end by an evil deed or wait for the Lord in confidence that He could and would establish him in his throne?[9] Not an easy choice when you are on the run and not sure about tomorrow.

Adding to the ethics of the moment is the contrast between the cave and camp narratives. They begin similarly and then go their separate ways. The cave experience depicts David's restraint when given an unexpected opportunity to harm or kill Saul. The camp incident illustrates David's ability to get himself in a position from which he could kill Saul. Now David is master and demonstrates his mastery by not acting. This is no chance encounter at Hachilah, as it was at En-gedi.[10]

Abishai rightly perceived that it was the Lord who had delivered the king into their hands, but he was wrong on what that situation meant or what to do with it. Undoubtedly God arranged for Saul to be at David's mercy, but not for the purpose of killing him. Rather, the Lord used the occasion to refine David's self-control, integrity, and trust in Himself further.[11] In keeping with the divine way of doing things, David restrained himself. He did not act in order to demonstrate his power or his ability to act. Instead, he simply chose to show in a dramatic and impressive manner that he could kill. But David did not harm Saul.[12]

Once again, David would not lift his hand against the Lord's anointed (1 Sam. 26:11). Nor would he permit Abishai to do so (verse 9). It was not that David shrank from the idea of Saul's death. David could quickly name opportunities for Abishai of how the king might die: by God's hand, by natural crisis, by battle wounds. Saul would surely perish—but not in any way that implicated David. Attentive to God, David understood this moment as an opportunity to demonstrate restraint and good will, not vengeance. Two years earlier David had taught his men that it was not right to touch the Lord's anointed. Once again he had to battle the powerful human impulse to get even. And once again he demonstrated a supreme moment of self-control. Faith on the run can do it right! Passion for God can override every other passion.

### Attacking the Heart

Abishai must have been really confused when David said, "The Lord forbid that I should stretch out my hand against the Lord's anointed; but now please take the spear that is at his head and the jug of water, and let us go" (verse 11, NASB). *This doesn't make sense!* he must have thought. *Risking our lives, we came all the way in here. Adrenaline surging at every snap of a twig. We got the king in our hands, and you only want to take the king's spear and water jug? Did we really come and risk everything just for that?*

When David asked, "Who will go down with me to Saul in the camp?" Abishai thought assassination was on the agenda. But David had another kind of attack in mind. He would thrust another kind of spear through Saul's heart. By piercing the moral heart of the king—touching his conscience—he wanted to see whether he might not at last move him to repentance. David sought to make it very clear that he was a faithful subject and devoted servant. That he did not harbor in his heart—even in the remotest degree—any evil intent toward him.[13]

David and Abishai accomplished their act of bravado in secrecy: "No one saw or knew about it, nor did anyone wake up. They were all sleeping, because the Lord had put them into a deep sleep " (verse 12, NIV). They crossed over to the other side of the valley and stood on top of the hill some distance away, making sure they had a good distance between themselves and Saul's camp. Then, in the predawn darkness, David's voice echoed across the canyon.

David first directed his attention to the king's military leader. "Wake up, Abner!"

"Who is it?" the officer demanded.

" 'Well, Abner, you're a great man, aren't you?' David taunted. 'Where in all Israel is there anyone as mighty? So why haven't you guarded your master the king when someone came to kill him? This isn't good at all! I swear by the Lord that you and your men deserve to die, because you failed to protect your master, the Lord's anointed! Look around! Where are the king's spear and the jug of water that were beside his head?' " (verses 14-16, NLT).

David thus mocked him with his incompetence. He must have had something in mind when he called out in the darkness to Abner. Abner was Saul's cousin, serving the king as his most important general for 24 years. He had been present when David slew Goliath and had the most to lose in terms of prestige and position during the time David was winning battles for Saul. Earlier, when David had spared Saul's life in the cave, he had told the king that someone was telling lies about him, poisoning Saul against him (1 Sam. 24:9). In light of the threat David posed to Abner's generalship, wasn't he the prime suspect for spreading such tales? Later, after Saul's death, Abner would spend seven years trying to pump life into a dying dynasty. One other thing seems suspicious about him. How did Abner survive the battle of Mount Gilboa when all the other ranking officers of Saul's inner circle perished along with the king and Jonathan?

By now Saul recognized David's voice. "Is that you, my son David?"

"Yes, my lord the king. Why are you chasing me? What have I done?

What is my crime? But now let my lord the king listen to his servant. If the Lord has stirred you up against me, then let him accept my offering. But if this is simply a human scheme, then may those involved be cursed by the Lord. For you have driven me from my home, so I can no longer live among the Lord's people and worship as I should. Must I die on foreign soil, far from the presence of the Lord? Why has the king of Israel come out to search for a single flea? Why does he hunt me down like a partridge on the mountains?" (1 Sam. 26:17-20, NLT).

"Then Saul confessed, 'I have sinned. Come back home, my son, and I will no longer try to harm you, for you valued my life today. I have been a fool and very, very wrong.'

"'Here is your spear, O king,' David replied. 'Let one of your young men come over and get it. The Lord gives his own reward for doing good and for being loyal, and I refused to kill you even when the Lord placed you in my power, for you are the Lord's anointed one. Now may the Lord value my life, even as I have valued yours today. May he rescue me from all my troubles'" (verses 21-24, NLT).

"And Saul said to David, 'Blessings on you, my son David. You will do heroic deeds and be a great conqueror'" (verse 25, NLT). Saul's last words to David were ones of blessing—a vindication of David's character and a prediction of his future.

Then David went away, and Saul returned home.

David's last recorded words to his royal father-in-law focus on the "law of spiritual sowing and reaping." Their major premise is that the Lord returns to individuals their righteousness and faithfulness (1 Sam. 26:23; Gal. 6:7). They also reveal how much David valued the life of Saul. He set a high worth on the king's *nephesh*, his soul or total being. The Hebrew term used here means "highly valued." This was not just "I'll be a good boy and not kill the king" kind of thing. David truly respected Saul. The king was not only the Lord's anointed, he was also a human being and his father-in-law. Because David valued the life of Saul, he could anticipate that God would honor his own life and deliver him from trouble (1 Sam. 26:24). David expected the Lord to reward him for his righteousness and regard his life as highly as he in turn did that of Saul.[14] Furthermore, David wanted to make it very clear that it was totally irrational for the king to seek his life when those who were on Saul's side weren't as concerned for his life as David was.[15]

In essence, David asserts that wrongdoing, righteousness, and faithfulness do matter. He and Saul live in a world of moral symmetry and may expect God to treat them according to their conduct.[16]

Interestingly, in light of how David demonstrated Saul's value in his sight, the king now also honors David. Saul concedes that he has acted foolishly (verse 21; as foolish as the fool [Nabal] in chapter 25). Then he blesses David. In light of David's integrity and the way he treated him, Saul could only respond in kind. Proverbs tells us that "when a man's ways are pleasing to the Lord, He makes even his enemies to be at peace with him" (Prov. 16:7, NASB). That's an incredible promise but not something that happens easily. Furthermore, it may not come true every time. It would be wonderful if every time you do what is right, your enemy would always see the error of his or her ways and quickly repent and view you correctly. Unfortunately it doesn't always occur that way. But it can take place more than it does now if we trust God and do things His way. The whole ending of this story involves the outworking of that principle. If it can occur between Saul and David, it can happen between you and someone with whom you are in conflict.

David's words open up to us a vital insight into his inmost being. Although the incident thoroughly humiliates Abner in front of the whole camp, all of Saul's soldiers—some whom had undoubtedly served previously with David when he was in the king's good graces—must have come to admire David as a man of tremendous character.[17] The episode honored God, displayed moral excellence, and revealed a better way. And perhaps most important of all, it maintained David's passion.

One of the features of this last exchange between the two men is the grace and patience of God's reaching out to the king through David. The Lord was using Saul to prepare David for leadership. At the same time, He was also confronting Saul with Himself through David. God was longsuffering toward the king. His mercy toward an undeserving man was gracious and great. Unfortunately even this flow of divine grace did not soften Saul to the point of full surrender.

After talking with the king, David returned to his wilderness hideaway and resumed his fugitive life. As before, he had no confidence in Saul's repentance.

This episode in David's fugitive years provides a tremendous lesson on power, restraint, opportunity, and ultimate trust in God. According to David, only the Lord had the right to lay a hand on Saul. Heroic as David's daring night escapade had been, its success had been possible thanks only to supernatural intervention and his underlying passion for God.[18]

And so we must ask ourselves, How do I handle compelling temptation when it comes around the second time? The very temptation I've already resisted and overcome? Circumstances may be different, but at bottom it's the same issue, the same enticement. Am I ready to deal with it? stronger? more determined to be faithful to God? Can I put myself in its way (not recommended) and not be swayed? When opportunity knocks, how do I respond? Do I assume that God is leading? When power is in my hand, how do I use it? Am I a terminator in heart—or like God? Where would the Holy Spirit develop restraint in my life? Where do I need to simply wait for God to accomplish His will—in His time and in His way? Am I willing to let Him proceed at His own pace?

"Wait for the Lord and keep His way,
 and He will exalt you to inherit the land;
When the wicked are cut off,
 you will see it."

         —Psalm 37:34, NASB

"Judge me, O Lord,
 according to my righteousness, according to my integrity,
 O Most High.
O righteous God, who searches minds and hearts,
 bring to an end the violence of the wicked and make the
 righteous secure.
My shield is God Most High, who saves the upright in heart."

         —Psalm 7:8-10, NIV

Be still, O heart! Wait for God. This will keep us from actions and words that, if allowed, would shadow our whole life. Live on the divine purpose. We must not be eager for ourselves, but only that God's way should be done. It's the only way to keep passion.

---

[1] Alden Thompson, *Samuel: From the Danger of Chaos to the Danger of Power* (Boise, Idaho: Pacific Press Pub. Assn., 1995), p. 169.

[2] Walter Brueggemann, *First and Second Samuel*, p. 182.

[3] Theodore Epp, *A Man After the Heart of God*, p. 81.

[4] Keith Kaynor, *When God Chooses: The Life of David,* p. 123.

[5] *Ibid.,* pp. 124, 125.

[6] Thompson, p. 169.

[7] Brueggemann, p. 184.

[8] Bill Powell and Yevgenia Albats, "The Man Who Would Be Tsar," *Newsweek,* Mar. 27, 2000, p. 42.

[9] Holmes Rolston, *Personalities Around David,* p. 62.

[10] Peter D. Miscall, *1 Samuel,* p. 158.

[11] Kaynor, p. 125.

[12] Miscall, p. 162.

[13] F. W. Krummacher, *David: King of Israel,* p. 153.

[14] Ralph W. Klein, *1 Samuel,* p. 260.

[15] Gene A. Getz, *David: Seeking God Faithfully,* p. 118.

[16] Brueggemann, p. 187.

[17] Kaynor, p. 126.

[18] Klein, p. 260.

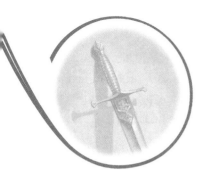

9

# LIVING WITH THE ENEMY

## I Samuel 27

Throughout history the crossing of rivers has symbolized an important personal experience. In Greek mythology the river Styx represented the boundary between life and death (the Jordan in Christian
imagery). And when Julius Caesar crossed the Rubicon, it marked his as-
cent to absolute leadership of the Roman Empire. The children of Israel's
crossings of the Red Sea and the Jordan River were incredible moments of
decision, transition, and experience (Ex. 14; 15; Joshua 3:1-17). When
David finally tired of running from Saul, he experienced an unforgettable
crossing: "So David arose and crossed over, he and the six hundred men
who were with him, to Achish the son of Maoch, king of Gath" (1 Sam.
27:2, NASB). Although the passage mentions no river here, there is a symbolic "crossing over" nevertheless.

Now, the Hebrew word *habar*—meaning "cross over" or to "pass
over"—implies the distinct line of demarcation between two positions.
This boundary line accentuates the decision and experience involved in
the shift from one point to the other. It implies crossing a boundary—
whether physical such as a valley or river (Deut. 2:13, 14); political, as
with a nation's border (verse 18); or moral, as to enter a covenant or
transgress a commandment (Deut. 29:12; 26:13; Joshua 7:11, 15). The
word connotes something with tremendous epic and existential signifi-

cance. The crossing over involves great spiritual and moral ramifications as well as the emotional and physical well-being of the individual. Whatever the choice, life will never be quite the same again.

Every life has its crossover times. Some people call them the "peak" experiences, but they are points of transition—often fraught with potential disaster. Such experiences can be frightening, growing, devastating, rejuvenating, exhilarating, or disillusioning. They are important moments of moral spiritual decision, experience, transition, or formation. Those most important decisions we make in life have that quality—for example, to open our lives to Jesus in repentance and receive His forgiveness and grace, to marry (and whom), what career track we take, to divorce or not, to accept that mission call or move to another state away from family and friends, etc. How we handle a crossover experience inevitably affects spiritual passion. And what we cross over to invariably measures it.

For David, that crossover boundary lay between the "land of the Philistines" and the "territory of Israel" (1 Sam. 27:1). His "crossing over" was a deliberate attempt to find asylum among the enemy.

Life on the run obviously had taken its toll. Fear, frustration, and exhaustion apparently left him feeling hopeless. The whole mess was tiring and discouraging. You can hear the downward spiral of his mood in his thought, "One of these days I will be destroyed by the hand of Saul" (verse 1, NIV). In his thinking, the only way to put an end to Saul's pathological game of hide-and-seek was to escape the king's sphere of control altogether. Saul knew all David's hiding places by now. The constant flight was hard on his men and their families. Food was difficult to scrounge up in the wilderness. Spies lurked everywhere. But everyone knew that Saul was afraid of the Philistines. David and his followers would be safe among them.

"Someday Saul is going to get me!" David wanted to settle down with his family. He wanted to be safe—at least for a while. Although he felt like giving up, he couldn't because everyone had become an enemy in his eyes. "The best thing I can do is to escape to the land of the Philistines," he said to himself. "Then Saul will give up searching for me anywhere in Israel, and I will slip out of his hand" (verse 1, NIV). David was thinking first and foremost of himself—his anxieties, his problems, his fears and feelings of rejection and abandonment.

Was there truly nothing better for him to do than to seek refuge with the Philistines? Why couldn't he remain in Judah, trusting in the One who had been a constant shield around him? He may have been living a fugitive's life, but again and again God had defied all human odds and delivered David and his vastly outnumbered band. Yet, instead of firming David's faith, such close calls and last-minute rescues left him exhausted.

*Patriarchs and Prophets* tells us that "David's conclusion that Saul would certainly accomplish his murderous purpose was formed without the counsel of God. Even while Saul was plotting and seeking to accomplish his destruction, the Lord was working to secure David the kingdom. God works out His plans, though to human eyes they are veiled in mystery. Men cannot understand the ways of God; and, looking at appearances, they interpret the trials and tests and provings that God permits to come upon them as things that are against them, and that will only work their ruin. Thus David looked on appearances, and not at the promises of God. He doubted that he would ever come to the throne. Long trials had wearied his faith and exhausted his patience."[1]

How long was God going to keep David on the run? We can understand how he might have slipped into a pit of despair, crying wearily to God:

"O Lord, how long will you forget me? Forever?
How long will you look the other way?
How long must I struggle with anguish in my soul,
    with sorrow in my heart every day?
How long will my enemy have the upper hand?"
—Psalm 13:1, 2, NLT

There is nothing ethically or spiritually wrong with those feelings of despair that chill us like an unexpected downpour. It is when we take matters into our own hands and flee to a cover of our own choosing that we further deplete our spiritual passion. Attempting to solve his problems by his own wits, David only complicated them. His self-spun web of trouble began subtly, almost innocently—"The best thing I can do is to escape to the land of the Philistines."

His mind made up, David "crossed over" into Philistia and presented himself to Achish, king of Gath. It was the second time he had gone to Gath for asylum. He was quite vulnerable and very much alone that first visit, so he had feigned madness as a way to escape. Now he was a leader of a formidable band of guerrilla warriors—one who might easily turn the scale of strength in the long struggle between Israel and Philistia. David was also an infamous outlaw—a would-be usurper of Saul's throne. The Israelite king so feared him that Saul had repeatedly sent thousands of men to the desert to track David down. The Philistines were well aware of the conflict and had often timed their raids to coincide with Saul's forays against David (1 Sam. 23:27, 28). Acting on the timeless dictum "My enemy's enemy is my friend," Achish welcomed the fugitive with open arms. Granting him asylum, though, was a considerable commitment, to say the least. David's entire group must have numbered more than 1,000 individuals. Each man had his family with him. David brought his two wives, Ahinoam and Abigail. His entourage was large enough to have disrupted life in Gath and created resentment among some of the city's residents.[2]

As David and his men settled in Gath word reached Saul that David had settled in Philistine territory. Just as David had hoped, the king stopped hunting him. His "crossover" plan had worked. But now he had to confront some of the realities of being in Gath. The size of his troop proved disrupting. They encountered different customs and culture and food. Gath was a stark pagan environment full of idols and idolatrous practices. Finally David asked Achish for another place to live—somewhere in the country, a city away from Gath. So Achish obliged. He gave him Ziklag, a city located about 25 miles southwest of Gath (1 Sam. 27:5-7).

When he "crossed over" into Philistia, David no doubt had merely a physical or territorial boundary in mind. It was just a place to get away from Saul. He had no conscious thought of moral or spiritual compromise with the Philistines. But in the process of cozying up to the invaders of Palestine, ingratiating himself with them, David unwittingly "crossed over" some spiritual moral boundaries as well. David could easily see the physical boundaries. But the subtle spiritual and moral boundaries, though just as real, he often found harder to recognize.

Boundaries define us. They designate what is me and what is not me. A boundary shows me where I end and someone else begins. Who I am. What I am like in terms of attitudes and beliefs, behaviors, choices, values, limits.[3] When I cross over a boundary, things get blurred inside, stretching spiritual passion and making my passion for God vulnerable.

The world of the Bible divided into two camps: Israel and the nations. One is holy, the other is impure. How many times had the Lord warned Israel never to develop relationships with pagan people? to keep separate and to guard their dealings? He didn't want them influenced by pagan values until the distinction between His people and the world became so blurred that one could no longer tell the difference. Nor did He want His people to learn the ways of their unbelieving neighbors. Crossing over to Philistia proved a highly injurious decision on David's part. Philistia was full of pagan temples and idolatrous priests (2 Sam. 5:21)

But for the first time in years David was free from the pressures of Saul's pursuit. It felt so good! He could overlook the in-your-face idolatry because he no longer needed to run.

### Master of Masks

Unfortunately, though, David wasn't as free as he had hoped. Friendship with Achish came with a price. As payment for his protection, Achish expected loyalty in return—and money! It was a heavy debt that David may not have bargained on. He had to adopt the Philistine cause. So while in Ziklag, David lived like a robber baron. He spent his time attacking and plundering vulnerable smaller settlements at will, making him a kind of Robin Hood, but without the moral high ground.[4] He was a freelance guerrilla warrior pursuing his own ends in the south.[5] By crossing over to Philistia he had plunged himself and his followers into an unseemly career of violence and deception.

"David and his men spent their time raiding the Geshurites, the Girzites, and the Amalekites—people who had lived near Shur, along the road to Egypt, since ancient times. David didn't leave one person alive in the villages he attacked. He took the sheep, cattle, donkeys, camels, and clothing before returning home to see King Achish" (1 Sam. 27:8, 9).

"'Where did you make your raid today?' Achish would ask.

"And David would reply, 'Against the south of Judah, the Jerahmeelites, and the Kenites'" (verse 10, NLT).

His men would leave no one alive to notify Gath where he had really been. He conducted such raids repeatedly while he was living among the Philistines.

"Achish believed David and thought to himself, 'By now the people of

Israel must hate him bitterly. Now he will have to stay here and serve me forever!'" (verse 12, NLT).

Thus David not only joined the enemy, he double-crossed it.[6] He pretended to have turned traitor to his own people, marauding and looting Israelite villages on a daily basis, while in actual fact massacring tribes to the south, longtime enemies of Israel. Then he brought back the plunder—identified to Achish as coming from Israelites—and shared it with the king. In order to prevent any report of his raids on the south, David adopted the cruel and murderous policy of leaving neither man nor woman alive. Dead men (and women and children) tell no tales!

One thing needs to be extremely clear at this point. In his raids among the pagan villages to the south David was not "fighting the battles of the Lord." He was securing his own position. His motive for allowing no one to remain alive was strictly personal.[7] In his day soldiers could sell their captives as slaves. Such slaves were normally the most profitable part of war booty. Achish, though, misinterpreted the absence of slaves in David's plunder as proof that he so hated his native people that he preferred killing them to selling them.[8] He imagined that David had burned his bridges to Israel and had made himself an enemy of his own people. Thus the warlord had no alternative but to remain in his service.

By trying to solve his own problems, David put himself in a highly precarious position. On the one hand, he had to keep Achish convinced that he was pro-Philistine. At the same time, he couldn't let the Hebrews think he was a traitor. To demonstrate loyalty to the Hebrews, he would raid Judah's enemies in the south. Then to protect himself from Achish, he skirted the truth by telling the king that he was attacking the south country of Judah, which led Achish to believe that David was actually fighting his own people. It was true that David was carrying out raids in the south—but which south?

David was a supersalesman![9] By this point in his life he was telling boldfaced lies. In the process he was sinking deeper and deeper into the mire of sin and walking further and further away from God's will. In Achish's eyes David was a deserter (1 Sam. 29:3). But by settling in enemy territory David became a traitor in the eyes of his own people as well. He gave the impression to his own people that he had gone to the pagans to serve their gods, thus providing opportunity for many to misconstrue his motives. His actions revealed the weaknesses of his own people and en-couraged the Philistines to relentlessly harass and oppress the land of Israel.[10] David gave advantage to the enemy and opened himself to a life of deceit and duplicity. When he practiced deception he was not walking in the counsel of God.[11]

At first he had a false sense of security. "I'm all right living with the enemy. I still keep my distance." But in essence David was advancing the enemy's cause. It all turned into a lengthy period of compromise—16 months of duplicity and vagueness. David's mind had to keep busy weav-ing a fabric of deceit and cruelty.[12] He more or less had to do whatever was necessary to survive. As a result we find him in great distress. Violence and brutality and deception seem the only way out.[13] Such a course would inevitably lead him straight out of God's will. God could never condone David's behavior or help him to achieve goals in opposi-tion to the divine will. It simply indicates how much we can accomplish with our own wisdom—and then rationalize it as proof that God is on our side. In the process spiritual passion wanes.

At this point in his life David typifies the person who may be a believer on the inside, but on the outside appears just like a nonbeliever because of lifestyle.[14] Too much "crossing over" has blurred the character and moral spiritual life. You can't be sure where David really stands anymore. When we cross boundaries we can become confused in our identity.

Scripture tells us that he took his family with him to Philistia. Do you think he could compromise and it not affect them? And do you think that you can "cross over" moral or spiritual boundaries and it not affect your own family? Think again. We do not live independently of everyone else. When we make a wrong decision it touches those who trust us and de-pend on us, those who look up to us and believe in us. Our sinful choices influence them. When we "cross over" they "cross over" too. Maybe not in the same exact way or at the same exact moment, but moral spiritual boundaries blur for them as well. All too often they go even further than we have.

Meyer puts it in perspective: "Their perpetual familiarity with the rites and iniquities of idolatry could not but exert an unwholesome and alto-gether disastrous effect on the minds of the unstable in his band. Poison must have been injected into many hearts that wrought disastrously in later years. What was harmless enough in the case of David, who knew that an idol was nothing in the world, was perilous in the extreme to the weak consciences to some of his men who were defiled by what they saw and heard."[15]

Let a Christian leader give in to the enemy in the midst of the pressures and battles of life, and the consequences are widespread. Some people are inwardly thankful when a Christian leader falls or compromises ("crosses over")! It gives them an excuse for compromise, of obtaining peace at any price.[16] Redpath warns that "if you desert to the devil in one issue of your life, he can turn the whole tide of the spiritual warfare in your community. That is what the deserter does: he gives the advantage to the enemy."[17] David was a deserter both in the sight of the Philistines and the eyes of many in Israel, and it had a disastrous effect on his men and their families. It opened the way for idolatry, duplicity, and compromise, making it easier for them to live to please themselves rather than honor God.

Redpath further notes that "it is a tragedy in the life of a child of God when he yields to the pressure of Satan, and God leaves him on his own. He is reduced to scheming and planning, and when he is driven into a tight corner he can escape only by deceit. Suddenly the man who has given in to depression realizes that he has purchased his deliverance from the pressure of the devil at too great a price. He has obtained release from tension for a moment, but he has exchanged the smile of God for the grin of the enemy. He has exchanged the protection of Jesus Christ for the flimsy walls of defeat, as David exchanged trust in the promises of God for the walls of Ziklag, which soon were going to be burned by fire and over which David would weep scalding, bitter tears of repentance. Oh, the harm that is done by a man who gives in to the enemy!"[18]

An advertisement boasting Epson Stylus Color Ink Jet Printers displayed a full-page spread of a herd of zebras. Because they were packed closely together, all you saw was a maze of stripes and heads or manes or rumps, but mostly the white and reddish-brown stripes. A little green box on the left read: "With ordinary printers you see the stripes on the zebra." A matching green box to the right declared: "With our printer you see the woman on the zebra." Suddenly you find yourself searching for the elusive woman that you missed in your first scan. Sure enough, she's there, wearing a zebra-colored hooded jumpsuit. The flesh tones of her face match the colors on the zebra's noses. Once you see her, she's easy to pick out. At first, though, you'd miss her for sure. "She's incredibly well camouflaged," the advertisement continues on the facing page. "But you can spot her. Unmistakably. And the company responsible for this sales report knew you would. Because the printer they created it on in its entirety—text and all—was an Epson. One with such acute attention to detail that, even with images as challenging as this, absolutely nothing gets lost in transition. So always, just as you see here, every color and shade is realized. Every nuance is captured. And as you'll discover, when it comes to printers, every stripe is earned."

When David "crossed over" he wound up living in lies, living by the sword, and siding with the enemy. He became incredibly camouflaged to everyone looking on—his fellow Israelites, the Philistines, King Achish. We can spot him, though. Unmistakably. Once we see him, we realize how far spiritual passion can plummet when we compromise boundaries.

### Why Do You Stand So Far Off, Lord?

It should have been a delightful Saturday morning excursion. Bryan Wolfe and his 2-year-old daughter, Brittany, were out for a drive in his Datsun pickup. His wife, Tracy, had just finished her night shift and was sound asleep back home. It would be several hours yet until he needed to show up for his shift at a plywood mill where he operated a forklift. Figuring he would be back before Tracy awoke, he didn't leave a note.

They drove down the highway near their Oregon home, then took a gravel road and after a few miles turned down a dirt lane. Shifting into four-wheel drive, Bryan picked his way through towering firs until they reached a clearing. It was about 10:30 a.m. A beaver pond sparkled in the sun. Bryan figured he could stay for about an hour before making the 14-mile drive home. For a while he and Britanny looked for beavers and splashed their hands in the water. It was a beautiful morning. The dense Oregon forest was peaceful. Birds called from giant trees, and patches of sunlight glowed on the pine-needle carpet.

As Bryan drank in the fresh air he caught himself thinking of the God who had created it all, then quickly shrugged the thought away. He had not been on speaking terms with God for a long time. The idea of obeying in everything wasn't that appealing to him. Besides, he figured, if he was ever to get anything out of this life it was up to him. So far he had done all right too. He had a good wife, a sweet daughter, and a decent job. Right then he was doing what he liked best, enjoying the outdoors.

Then remembering the new rifle hanging in the cab of the pickup, Bryan decided to try it out. Putting Britanny in her carseat to keep her out of the way and safe, he picked up a quart-sized plastic bottle that was lying nearby and filled it with pond water. He also found an empty beer can. Some 60 yards from the truck loomed an old gray-red Douglas fir stump that loggers had left behind. It stood more than six feet high and must have been at least 15 feet around. An earthen bank behind it offered a perfect safety buffer. So Bryan set the bottle and can on the hollow stump's rim, went back to the truck, rested his rifle on the hood, and picked both off with one shot each. It felt good. The rifle zeroed in just right.

His targets had toppled down inside the trunk. Curious to see where he had hit them, Bryan set the rifle on the hood, then went and leaned over the stump's rim. Balancing on his stomach, he reached way down to retrieve his targets when *crack!* The rotted wood crumbled under him, and he plummeted headfirst into the hollow stump. He had dropped three quarters of the way down, and his right hand had caught between the wood and his body. But he could use his left. He started pushing when *whump,* he slipped all the way into the stump. His head now was smack against the bottom, his right arm still trapped.

*Now I'm really in trouble,* he thought. It was Saturday. No one he knew of was going to be around. Gritting his teeth, he tried to push himself up, then hook his toes over the stump's rim to hoist his body. But it was hopeless. He was wedged like a cork in a bottle. As he slumped down, panting heavily, the pungent odor of rotted wood filled his nostrils. Blood pounded in his head. Sweat burned his eyes. Panic began to flood him as he fought claustrophobia. As he struggled to free himself again, he heard a sound that froze him. "Da-da? Da-da?" Britanny had climbed out of her car seat and was toddling around looking for her father. She could fall into the beaver pond. Like a trapped tiger, Bryan struggled in blind fury, but the jagged wood bit into his body, only imprisoning him tighter.

"Britanny!" he cried. "Stay by the truck!" But the thick-walled stump muffled his voice.

In terror Bryan continued to struggle. As rotted wood crumbled under his flailing left hand, he thought, *This is it! I will dig myself out.* Clawing viciously at the moldy porous wood, he sought to open a hole large enough to wiggle out. But cruel reality struck when his fingernails hit the trunk's hard outer wood.

Panting, he collapsed again. Wood dust half blinded him. Thirsty and desperate, he felt insects crawling all over his face. The humid heat, stench, and being upside down made him nauseous. Bile burned in his throat, and he wanted to vomit. While coughing, spitting, and brushing ants from his sweating face, Bryan realized he had not heard Britanny for a long time. What had happened to her?

"O God," he cried, "please take care of my little girl. She is so innocent. Take me instead, a sinner, but save her." Then he broke down and sobbed, "Please forgive me for turning my back on You." Finally, succumbing to his plight, he lost all control, screaming from deep within his soul until his throat was raw and he could only gasp for God to forgive his sins.[19]

Can you imagine Bryan trapped upside down like a cork in a bottle in a rotted tree stump? *Now I'm really in trouble!* he had thought, and he was.

That's how David felt. Trapped! Like he was really in trouble, wedged upside down like a cork in a bottle in a rotted tree stump. While others might overlook him because of his compromising, dissembling camouflage, David's interior world would always spot himself. Conscience was still at work.

The whole experience of David while in Philistia was utterly unworthy of his high character as God's anointed servant. It was also a barren time in his religious experience. The biblical narrative does not have David mentioning God while he was with Achish, even though Achish refers to both God (1 Sam. 29:9) and the Lord (verse 6).[20] The Bible credits no psalms to this period. Israel's sweet singer was mute. How could David sing the Lord's songs in a strange land while living in duplicity, compromise, and violence? When we turn to expediency, give in to depression, lie or live a lie, it silences the song of our heart. Spiritual passion loses its creativity and freshness when we cross boundaries. Art no longer fills our heart—only shame and guilt.

A couple psalms depict the growing sadness and depression that likely marked this period of David's life. I think of his soul-wrenching words of Psalm 10: "O Lord, why do you stand so far away? Why do you hide when I need you the most?" (verse 1, NLT). I think, too, of his despairing cry of loneliness in Psalm 22: "My God, my God! Why have you forsaken me? Why do you remain so distant? Why do you ignore my cries for help? Every day I call to you, my God, but you do not answer. Every night you hear my voice, but I find no relief" (verses 1, 2, NLT). Psalm 69 expresses the feelings of entrapment we feel when there's no way out but God: "Save me, O God, for the floodwaters are up to my neck. Deeper and deeper I sink into the mire; I can't find a foothold to stand on. I am in deep water, and the floods overwhelm me. I am exhausted from crying for help; my throat is parched and dry. My eyes are swollen with weeping, waiting for my God to help me. . . . O God, you know how foolish I am; my sins cannot be hidden from you. Don't let those who trust in you stumble because of me, O Sovereign Lord Almighty. Don't let me cause them to be humiliated, O God of Israel" (verses 1-6, NLT). Such psalms touch the profoundest sense of sorrow and existential angst. I think back to those haunting words of Psalm 13 we explored earlier:

"O Lord, how long will you forget me? Forever?
How long will you look the other way?
How long must I struggle with anguish in my soul,
    with sorrow in my heart every day?
How long will my enemy have the upper hand?"
                           —Psalm 13:1, 2, NLT

"How long must I struggle with anguish in my soul, with sorrow in my heart?" he cries. David spent 16 months passing through a dark spiritual forest. The tangled overgrowth hid the sun. Despairing of ever emerging, he is restless inside. *God has forgotten me—forever,* he thinks. *God doesn't care about me. I'm going to have to work things out for myself.*

Have you ever faced a conflict so serious and painful that you made a decision that eventually left you in a worse state than before? Your initial decision seemed so logical—so rational! It seemed like the only thing to do. At first, things went better. You felt great. But in the course of time you realized that you only dug yourself deeper, and God seemed so much farther away.[21] What was your spiritual passion quotient like then?

Are you a believer on the inside, but on the outside you want to look like the rest of the world? Does your life lack absolute allegiance? How do you feel about it?

Driven into tight corners, we often escape by deception and duplicity, purchasing our deliverance from the pressure of adverse circumstances with compromise. When we give in to Satan at any point in our life, we will have an immediate release from the pressure. In the course of time, though, we will find ourself entangled in ways that bring far more pain.[22] When we try to live peaceably with that which is sinful, it will always come back to haunt us. It cannot be done! Spiritual passion cannot survive in it.

Tragically, many men and women are living in Philistia under the patronage of Achish of Gath. They feel terrible and guilty about it, but they do not know what else they can do. Perhaps they hold down jobs in settings that are in defiant contempt of God's values or they choose spouses who do not love God and who hate the name of Jesus. Many find themselves inextricably tangled in an economic system that exploits the poor or ignores the oppressed. Others do their best to honor parents who dishonor God in thought, word, and deed. There is hardly a one of us who at one time or another in our life has not lived under Achish of Gath.

The peace David experienced in Philistia was a false one, and he paid an extremely heavy price for it. Although when he moved into enemy territory Satan "got off his neck" so to speak, as long as David was out of the will of God, the victory belonged to the devil.[23]

## I Will Receive You!

David had been a spiritual giant in the stories of 1 Samuel 26, but he shrinks in chapters 27 and 29. The David/Achish episode is not a biblical license for caving in to contemporary culture. Rather, it is a story of God's hidden providence. It offers a glimpse into God's behind-the-scenes efforts, revealing that He is doing for us what we are not doing for ourselves.[24]

This tragic moment in David's fugitive years started with David saying to himself "there is nothing better for *me*" (1 Sam. 27:1, NASB). God didn't tell him to go to Philistia. The Lord never sent him to seek protection among Israel's most bitter foes. Nor was David taking in God's viewpoint at this moment. Instead of asking for God's help, he followed his own heart. Exhausted, he made his decisions by his gut, his fears. His conclusion that Saul eventually was going to kill him directly contradicted what God had promised. It was a human viewpoint. David did not wait on the Lord. Lack of faith led him to "cross over" from the territory of Israel to Philistine territory. And David's unbelief dishonored God.

"Don't link up with unbelievers and try to work with them," the apostle Paul cautions. "What common interest can there be between goodness and evil? How can light and darkness share life together? How can there be harmony between Christ and the devil? What can a believer have in common with an unbeliever? What common ground can idols hold with the temple of God? For we, remember, are ourselves temples of the living God, as God has said: I will dwell in them and walk in them: and I will be their God, and they shall be my people. Therefore, come ye out from among them and be ye separate, saith the Lord, and touch no unclean thing; and I will receive you, and will be to you a Father, and ye shall be to me sons and daughters, saith the Lord Almighty.

"With these promises ringing in our ears, dear friends, let us cleanse ourselves from anything that pollutes body or soul. Let us prove our reverence for God by consecrating ourselves to him completely" (2 Cor. 6:14–7:1, Phillips).

---

[1] Ellen G. White, *Patriarchs and Prophets*, p. 672.
[2] Robert D. Bergen, *1, 2 Samuel*, p. 260.
[3] Henry Cloud and John Townsend, *Boundaries: When to Say Yes, When to Say No, to Take Control of Your Life* (Grand Rapids: Zondervan Publishing House, 1992), pp. 27-48.
[4] Alden Thompson, *Samuel: From the Danger of Chaos to the Danger of Power*, p. 171.
[5] Walter Brueggemann, *First and Second Samuel*, p. 188.
[6] Eugene Peterson, *Leap Over a Wall*, p. 97.
[7] Peter D. Miscall, *1 Samuel: A Literary Reading*, p. 165.
[8] Paul T. Gibbs, *David and His Mighty Men* (Washington, D.C.: Review and Herald Pub. Assn., 1970), p. 66.
[9] Gene A. Getz, *David: Seeking God Faithfully*, p. 139.
[10] White, *Patriarchs and Prophets*, pp. 672, 673.
[11] *Ibid.*, p. 673.
[12] F. B. Meyer, *The Life of David*, p. 115.
[13] Miscall, p. 166.
[14] C. R. Swindoll, *David: A Man of Passion and Destiny*, p. 110.
[15] Meyer, p. 114.
[16] Alan Redpath, *The Making of a Man of God: Studies in the Life of David*, p. 117.
[17] *Ibid.*

[18] *Ibid.*, p. 118.
[19] Bryan Wolfe, "My Tree-Stump Ordeal," *Guideposts*, February 1998, pp. 14-16.
[20] Miscall, p. 163.
[21] Getz, p. 134.
[22] Redpath, p. 115.
[23] Theodore Epp, *A Man After the Heart of God*, p. 87.
[24] Peterson, p. 99.

10

# WHEN YOUR ROOF CAVES IN

## I Samuel 30:1-8

It's a story of paradox. A scenic walk that turned deadly, drowning hikers in the desert. That's right—in the desert.

In the northern reaches of Arizona the endless vistas draw a procession of adventurers. But in August 1997 a dozen hikers headed to a place where they were cut off from the wide expanse of desert sky above them. Their destination: the lower Antelope Canyon, a bizarre and beautiful maze of sandstone walls that, at points, is some 100 feet deep and so narrow that hikers can touch both walls. It is a slit through time and nature, a crack in the earth. And for 11 adventurers, it was also a crypt. In the ultimate contradiction, these desert hikers, with their sunscreen and water bottles, drowned—overwhelmed by a flash flood that swept through the bone-dry canyon.

Disaster had come unexpectedly. Unbeknown to the hikers, a thunderstorm 15 miles to the south and 2,000 feet higher than the canyon itself was filling the rift with hail and rain. The torrent surged down it. When the deluge roared into sight the hikers faced a wall of mud, rocks, and water, and nowhere to go. Only one survived.[1]

The story of Ziklag begins with disaster that follows a narrow escape.

For a time David seemingly sidestepped the traps he had created for himself in Philistia. His mind was constantly at work as he had to cover his tracks continually. Eventually, however, he wasn't wise enough to come up with the solution to every problem he faced. His first real dilemma came when King Achish decided to make war against Israel: "In those days the Philistines gathered their forces to fight against Israel. Achish said to David, 'You must understand that you and your men will accompany me in the army.' David said, 'Then you will see for yourself what your servant can do.' Achish replied, 'Very well, I will make you my bodyguard for life'" (1 Sam. 28:1, 2, NIV).

David had done such a great job establishing his credibility with Achish that the king wanted the guerrilla chieftain to go into battle with him. Imagine his surprise when Achish told him he wanted to make him his personal bodyguard. What was he to do? It was a critical moment when David's body language, eye contact, and voice needed to be under total control. He could only nod affirmatively. To tell the truth now would mean suicide—not only for himself and his wives, but for his men and their families. Furthermore, he had become so indebted to the Philistine ruler that it was impossible to back out. His only choice was to feign excitement about the prospect of going into battle against Israel—and to hope that he could somehow get out of the mess he'd created for himself.

Fortunately a way out of his nerve-racking predicament came when the Philistine military leaders became skeptical. The troops were marching past their commanders in groups of a hundred and a thousand. When David and his men went by at the end with King Achish, their presence stunned the officers. "What are these worthless Israelites doing here?" they snarled to one another (1 Sam. 29:3, CEV). In their opinion, David had snowed Achish big-time. Having a more objective view of the situation, they had not forgotten the little ditty the women of Israel had sung about Saul who had slain his thousands and David his ten thousands. Nor had they any intention of becoming ten thousand and one. It was not a moment to keep quiet. Angrily they insisted that David and his army not join them in the fight against Israel, lest he seize the opportunity to make an inside attack on the Philistines during the coming battle against Saul. What better way, they reasoned, could David regain merit in the Israelite king's eyes (verse 4).

I find Achish's response most intriguing: "David used to be one of Saul's officers, but he left Saul and joined my army a long time ago. I've never had even one complaint against him" (verse 3, CEV). In other words, "Hey, everything's OK. David's our guy now. Don't worry. He's one of us!" Later Achish regretfully breaks the news to David, saying, "I swear by the living God of Israel that you have been loyal to me, and I would be pleased to have you go with me and fight in this battle. I have not found any fault in you from the day you came over to me. But the other kings don't approve of you. So go back home in peace, and don't do anything that would displease them" (verses 6, 7, TEV).

Obviously David had to lie again. He had to act surprised and disappointed that he couldn't continue to prepare for the battle against Israel.

"But what have I done?" he says. "Do you know anything I've ever done that would keep me from fighting the enemies of my king?" (verse 8, CEV).

"I believe that you're as good as an angel of God," Achish answers, "but our army commanders have decided that you can't fight in this battle. You and your troops will have to go back to the town I gave you. Get up and leave tomorrow morning as soon as it's light. I am pleased with you, so don't let any of this bother you" (verses 9, 10, CEV).

David had lied so well, had "crossed over" so convincingly, that Achish trusted him completely. Everything the guerrilla band leader said, he believed. David was a trusted servant. As good as an angel of God. Can you imagine? A pagan king employing imagery of integrity based on Israel's God. What a fake David had become! So much so that Achish's view of God was David's supposed integrity. The Israelite refugee had become a master prevaricator, a supersalesman who adjusted reality to his advantage. When a rock starts rolling down downhill, it gains momentum. This is what David found with regard to his lies. They just came tumbling out more and more. That's how it is when we allow dishonesty to creep into our lives. Our first scheme may include just a little white lie, but our next step leads to a bold-faced one. Before we know it, we're in so deep we're feigning something we're not. We've moved from telling lies to living them.

What a paradox that Achish twice referred to Israel's God in connection with David's supposed integrity. He viewed him as an "angel of God." As a pagan who worshiped many gods, embracing another "god" (including the God of Israel) was no big thing. If it could help achieve his goals, the more gods the better! There was safety in supernatural numbers. How ironic that the one David lied to would refer to the God of heaven in the context of David's integrity, honesty, and character. Surely the words of the pagan king must have pressed David's conscience to the quick. "The reply of Achish must have sent a chill of shame and remorse through David's heart, as he thought how unworthy of a servant of God were the deceptions to which he had stooped."[2]

Perhaps such things troubled his mind years later when he wrote about the character of those who would have fellowship with God: "He who walks with integrity, and works righteousness, and speaks truth in his heart" (Ps. 15:2, NASB). David certainly knew by experience that we need to watch our walk and our talk if we would have fellowship with God. Lying lips jeopardize spiritual passion. I believe he later realized his own personal weakness for telling lies. He certainly understood the nature of deceit and what it meant to be on the other end of a lying tongue (Ps. 12; 52; 64) and how it drained him of spiritual passion, creating a loss of spiritual power and moral equilibrium. Those discerning David's hand in Psalm 119 can imagine the passion of his heart as he prayed earnestly, "Remove from me the way of lying" (verse 29, NKJV).

What would you do if you found yourself on a dead-end street? Just park there endlessly? No, you would maneuver your car to a through street. Lying lips—a life of duplicity—is a dead-end street. David's passion for God could not survive this kind of life for long.

Tragically, David had "crossed over" so thoroughly in the eyes of the world that the nature and character of God Himself had become confused in the minds of those who were victims of his duplicity and deception. That is what compromise does. It blurs issues of truth and the character of God in the eyes of the people who observe us. Not only do we lose our sense of identity—Who am I? What is my mission? Where am I going? What's all of this about, this stuff I believed all my life? Who has my true allegiance? And spiritual passion?—but the people who witness our "crossing over" become confused and uncertain about important spiritual moral things as well. It undermines their passion for God as well. As with David, who had essentially lost his identity as an Israelite, those of us who carry the name of God but fail to act like the one whose name we bear, create confusion and disillusionment for those who have yet to believe.

By now David must have been inwardly breathing a sigh of relief. Yet we can only wonder what else was going on in his heart as he packed his bags and started home to Ziklag. Unbeknown to him, he was about to reap the results of his duplicity and sin.

## The Roof Caves In

Cresting the hill before Ziklag, David's men expected to see their families again and to enjoy the comforts of home. They had not rushed the return trip from Aphek, where they had camped with the Philistine armies, taking it rather in two days and a portion of a third. As they traveled some 55 miles to Ziklag they were no doubt elated and relieved at escaping from a treasonous encounter with their fellow Israelites. However, their upbeat mood instantly vanished when they arrived home.[3] Instead of loved ones watching for the expected warriors, David and his men found only charred ruins and trails of smoke spiraling skyward. Utter silence greeted them. During David's absence the Amalekites had struck with a vengeance (1 Sam. 30:1, 2). Their attack on David's base of operations was no doubt in retaliation for the assaults he and his men had conducted against their settlements during the past 16 months. They likely timed their raid to coincide with David's expected northern tour of duty with the Philistine armies against Israel. The Amalekites burned Ziklag to the ground. Unlike David, they captured the women and children, taking them alive with them when they left.

Tragedy rivaling that of Job was multiplied more than 600 times as everyone discovered the loss of all their possessions and the disappearance of their spouses and children. It so overwhelmed them that David and his men—some of the toughest men on the planet—wept until exhausted (verse 4). Scripture tells us that they continued to do so until they had no strength left in them to cry at all. As they speculated about the abuse and pain their wives and children may have faced at the hand of the Amalekites, their exhausted sorrow turned to bitterness and anger. That rage quickly focused on David. It was his fault, they began thinking. He had gotten them into this mess. His lies, his duplicity had led to this disaster. Talk of stoning him began to circulate (verse 6). Hurting people often find someone to blame. When we've suffered a loss, just as with David's men, we begin to look for stones to throw—and someone at whom to hurl them. David cried the same tears the other men did, but because they needed someone to blame, they focused their anger on him. In reality, he indeed was to blame!

At this point he seemed cut off from every human support. Forces beyond his control had swept from him all that he held dear on earth. Saul had driven him from his country. The Philistines had expelled him from their camp. The Amalekites had plundered his home. His wives and children were gone—either dead or enslaved. Now his own friends had banded against him and threatened to stone him. Where do you go in a time like this? Talk about faith on the run—passion in retreat!

Scripture tells us that David was "greatly distressed" (verse 6, NIV). Literally, he was "in a very tight place." The Hebrew points to the strong emotional response and inner turmoil that one experiences when pressed externally by enemies or internally by difficult or wrong decisions. Mutiny was in the making, and David was not sure what to do. Without doubt, it was one of the lowest moments of his life. His roof had caved in. He had hit rock bottom—again! Just at the moment when his prospects seemed to be improving, things once more turned bad! All was lost—irreparably! His double life had finally caught up with him.[4] Up to this point a great deal of David's problems and trials had come at the hands of others. Now, however, he was fully responsible for everything, as his men well knew.

At this moment David had to drink a bitter cup that he had never tasted before. Reaching the end of his resources, he stood alone, abandoned by his men.[5] Weakness is an important theme in this particular episode in David's life, and for the first time it attached to David himself.[6] Now David experienced the horror of being without divine protection. God had miraculously taken care of him on many other occasions, but the Lord had obviously removed that protection for the time being.[7]

In October 1999 a Learjet carrying champion golfer Payne Stewart and at least four other people flew a ghostly journey halfway across the United States. With its windows iced over and its occupants apparently incapacitated, the sleek Lear spiraled nosefirst into a grassy field when it ran out of fuel. Everyone aboard perished.[8]

The chartered twin-engine Lear 35 may have suddenly lost cabin pressure soon after taking off from Orlando for Dallas. Air-traffic controllers couldn't raise anyone by radio. Fighter jets sent after the plane followed it for much of its flight but were unable to help. They observed that the windows were frosted over, indicating the temperature inside was below freezing. Set on autopilot, the plane cruised 1,500 miles straight up the nation's midsection, across a half dozen states. Its porpoising altitude fluctuated between 22,000 and 45,000 feet before it ran out of fuel some four hours later and crashed in South Dakota.

Planes that fly above 12,000 feet are pressurized, because the air at such altitudes is too thin to breathe. When a plane loses pressure, those aboard slowly lose consciousness. If an aircraft had a door or window seal break, they could perish in seconds from lack of oxygen. At 40,000 feet the lesser outside air pressure can suck the oxygen out of a plane in as little as 20 seconds. At 30,000 the occupants may have two minutes. Oxygen masks hang at the outside shoulder of each pilot. If the cabin loses pressure suddenly, pilots can put them on in seconds, then quickly dive to a safe altitude before their passengers pass out. More insidious is a slow leak, allowing hypoxia, the lack of oxygen, to incapacitate everyone gradually.

To the uninformed looking upward, Stewart's ghostly flight looked normal. Just another one of those beautiful sleek Lears cruising high and fast through the sky. Lucky guys! If you were standing on the ground as it flew westward, you would not have known that anything was wrong inside. You might even have wished you were important enough to enjoy such a ride. Every external sign would suggest a straight-and-true course. But there was something drastically wrong inside. Everyone was dead. And it was only a matter of time until the aircraft crashed.

A similar pattern is often true in our lives. We fly high and fast, every external sign suggesting a straight-and-true course—spiritual passion. But the high stakes of living with the enemy can suck our spiritual oxygen out of us, leaving us drowsy, poor in judgment, morally and spiritually impaired, and filled with moral failures. We die inside. Then crash.

When we abandon God's will for us, trouble lies ahead. It may come suddenly or gradually, but eventually it will happen. And it often multiplies rapidly. "Crossing over" will always come back to haunt us! We will eventually reap what we sow. Nothing can put off the consequences of our decisions and actions forever. Living a life of lies, David was slowly dying inside and spiraling toward a fatal crash.

### Never Too Late!

When Bryan Wolfe found himself wedged upside down in a rotting tree trunk—stuck like a cork in a bottle—he tried desperately to get out, but couldn't. *Now I'm really in trouble!* he thought, and he was. Half blinded by wood dust and thirsty, he was coughing, spitting, and brushing ants from his sweating face. And he was worried about his daughter Britanny's safety. What had happened to her?

"O God," he cried, "please take care of my little girl. She is so innocent. Take me instead, a sinner, but save her." Then he broke down and sobbed, "Please forgive me for turning my back on You." Then, succumbing to his plight, he lost all control, screaming from deep within his soul until his throat was raw and he could only beg God to forgive his sins.

It was then that the words "The Lord is my shepherd" began running through his mind. He had recited the twenty-third psalm as a child. Now again and again he found himself mumbling, "The Lord is my shepherd . . . the Lord is . . ." Then he sank into oblivion.

Gradually the sound of a man's voice aroused him. "Hey, buddy, you want some help?"

Was he hallucinating? No, he heard the voice again. Someone was there!

"Yes, please . . . help . . . me," he groaned.

Strong arms grabbed Bryan's boots and lifted him up from the stump. Reeling, he couldn't stand. His swollen head felt like a pumpkin. Two men comforted him and called 9-1-1 for an ambulance. Then he remembered his daughter. "Britanny!" he rasped. "Britanny!"

One of the men carried her over to him. She was peacefully asleep. When he looked at his watch, it was 5:45 p.m. He had been stuck in the stump for more than six hours.

"What? How?" he gasped, turning to his rescuers. The men introduced themselves as forestry workers. They had parked a bulldozer a distance away and for some reason felt led to walk down to the clearing.

"We saw your truck," one of them said, "but didn't pay it much attention. We were about to leave when we spotted the rifle across the hood. That got us looking around, and there was your little girl asleep in a mossy ditch. When we saw your boots we figured at first someone had left them resting on the stump and gone swimming.

"The Lord was watching over you both," he added.

Not until later did Bryan realize how much of a shepherd the Lord had been. He had led Britanny to a safe place and kept him alive until the two men arrived. As Bryan tells it, it took being stuck upside down in that tree stump—helpless—to get him to admit that he needed God. That he couldn't get everything out of life on his own.[9]

In the chaos of this desperate moment in David's life—in which lamentation, anger, and bitterness stirred dark passions of murder—we come to this incredible line: "But David strengthened himself in the Lord his God" (1 Sam. 30:6, NKJV). When David reached his lowest point—when he had nowhere to turn and his own self-centered strategies ultimately failed—he "strengthened himself in the Lord his God." For the first time in 16 months, David looks up and honestly says, "O, God, help me." Ellen White tells us that "though David, losing his grasp on divine power, had faltered and turned aside from the path of strict integrity, it was still the purpose of his heart to be true to God."[10]

David prayed. David worshiped. And David called his pastor, Abiathar, for counsel. Delving deep within himself—to meet God—he found strength and direction to rise up from the ashes of his broken life. As his exterior world collapsed, he returned to the interior and rebuilt his primary identity. For 16 months David had been under Achish's thumb. Now the future king of Israel was dealing with God again. Confessing. Listening intently. Choosing to trust and obey once more.[11] Point by point he reviewed his past eventful life. Where had the Lord ever forsaken him? Recalling the many evidences of God's favor now refreshed his spiritual life. Though he himself could not discern a way out of the difficulty, God could see it and would teach him what to do.[12]

David and Abiathar came out from the place of quietness and counsel and prayer with a plan.[13] David had asked God, "Shall I pursue this band? Shall I overtake them?" And God answered, "Pursue, for you shall surely overtake them, and you shall surely rescue all" (verse 8, NASB). Not only does God hear, but He answers with a promise. The Lord vowed that David would recover all. And that's exactly what happened. David regained everything—not only his loved ones and material possessions, but also his spiritual vision, passion, and action.[14] He charged off so fast that one third of his 600 men became weary and had to remain behind a short way down the trail. The restored zeal of their leader wore them out.[15] They couldn't keep up with David.

Amazingly, when David repented, he recovered in a day what he had lost during a period of months and years. When he turned back to the Lord, Heaven answered him immediately. And the Lord will respond instantly if we meet His conditions. "We must never conclude that it's too late to turn back to God."[16] Though we may have to reap what we have sown, God's grace and forgiveness are always available to all who call on Him. Isaiah promises us that the Lord is with those who are of a humble and contrite heart (Isa. 57:15). "Everyone who calls on the name of the Lord will be saved" (Rom. 10:13, NIV). "If we confess our sins, he is faithful and just to forgive us our sins, and to cleanse us from all unrighteousness" (1 John 1:9).

God's grace is amazing! In spite of David's duplicity and compromise—in spite of the web of sin he had entangled himself in, his "crossing over" and blurring his identity as a follower of God—the Lord began to provide a way out of the quagmire he David had created. "The Lord in His great mercy did not punish this error of His servant by leaving him to himself in his distress and perplexity. . . . While Satan and his host were busy helping the adversaries of God and of Israel to plan against a king who had forsaken God, the angels of the Lord were working to deliver David from the peril into which he had fallen. Heavenly messengers moved upon the Philistine princes to protest against the presence of David and his force with the army in the approaching conflict. . . . Thus the snare in which David had become entangled was broken, and he was set free."[17]

In His grace God had allowed the Amalekites to plunder Ziklag in order to chasten David for the lack of faith that had led him to place himself among the Philistines and feel secure in the midst of his enemies.[18] "When David had invaded the territory of the Amalekites, he had put to the sword all the inhabitants that fell into his hands. But for the restraining power of God the Amalekites would have retaliated by destroying the people of Ziklag. They decided to spare the captives, desiring to heighten the honor of the triumph by leading home a large number of prisoners, and intending afterward to sell them as slaves. Thus, unwittingly, they fulfilled God's purpose, keeping the prisoners unharmed, to be restored to their husbands and fathers."[19] In His gracious providence the chance illness of an Egyptian slave proved to be the key to David's victory and recovery of all losses.[20] God's providence gets David out of trouble, yet allows Ziklag to be burned and the Egyptian slave to get sick so that David could recover all and restore his spiritual passion. Through it all God was at work behind the scenes.

[1] "Drowning in the Desert," *Newsweek,* Aug. 25, 1997, p. 33.

[2] Ellen G. White, *Patriarchs and Prophets,* p. 691.

[3] Robert D. Bergen, *1, 2 Samuel,* p. 275.

[4] Keith Kaynor, *When God Chooses: The Life of David,* p. 136.

[5] Theodore H. Epp, *A Man After the Heart of God,* p. 99.

[6] Peter D. Miscall, *1 Samuel: A Literary Reading,* p. 179.

[7] Epp, p. 98.

[8] "A Learjet's Tragic Flight," *Newsweek,* Nov. 8, 1999, p. 38.

[9] Bryan Wolfe, "My Tree-Stump Ordeal," pp. 14-16.

[10] White, *Patriarchs and Prophets,* p. 690.

[11] Eugene Peterson, *Leap Over a Wall,* p. 105.

[12] White, *Patriarchs and Prophets,* pp. 692, 693.

[13] Peterson, p. 105.

[14] Alan Redpath, *The Making of a Man of God: Studies in the Life of David,* p. 134.

[15] Kaynor, p. 139.

[16] Gene A. Getz, *David: Seeking God Faithfully,* p. 145.

[17] White, *Patriarchs and Prophets,* pp. 690, 691.

[18] *Ibid.,* p. 692.

[19] *Ibid.,* pp. 693, 694.

[20] Kaynor, p. 139.

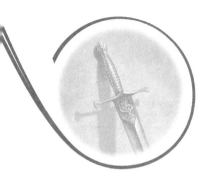

# NIGHT OF THE LIVING DEAD

## I Samuel 28:3-25

During October of 1997 three young actors went into the woods near Burkittsville, Maryland, to perform in a horror movie. Shot entirely on jumpy handheld cameras, for a budget that would barely buy a new car, the movie offered a grabbing premise: three film students disappear while shooting a documentary about the legend of a local witch who for two centuries has lured children to her home and, so the tale goes, made some of them face a wall while she killed the others. A year later someone finds their horrifying footage.

For eight days and nights the three actors camped in the woods, getting dirtier and hungrier as they filmed one another. In lieu of a script, each morning they each received private messages in film canisters and were told not to share them with the others. Hungry, exhausted, and increasingly isolated from one another and the outside world, the actors endured intense psychological pressure. Their production managers lurked in the eerie night shadows, creating noises, rattling their tent, and leaving ominous occult symbols and other creepy paraphernalia.

The upshot was three young people utterly spooked and scared out of their wits filming one another's unscripted involuntary fear and desperation. Interestingly, the film viewer never sees anything horrible. The movie has no scary creatures or bloodcurdling scenes. You just see three kids literally frightened to death. As you get drawn into their rising psycho-horror and desperation, it involuntarily evokes your own fear.

Twenty-two months later *The Blair Witch Project* was a smash—storming both the box office and the national pop consciousness. The quiet little town of Burkittsville (population: 214), whose only attraction up till then had been its historic Civil War battlegrounds, suddenly found itself overrun by fans wanting to visit its now-famous graveyard and tramp around in the woods trying to catch a glimpse of the Blair Witch for themselves. Many still think it is a true story. When you tell them it is all concocted, they assume there's a conspiracy and cover-up.[1]

In the wake of the *Blair Witch* phenomenon, an already high interest in witches and the occult naturally intensified. *Blair Witch* was more than a horror movie. It was a vivid expression of our culture's incessant fascination with the supernatural—the magical, the psychic, the occult, the dead, and demons and angels. The image of people flocking to a rundown graveyard in a previously unknown town to rub tombstones and tramp around in the nearby woods looking for a witch speaks volumes!

How pervasive is our world's preoccupation with such things? Take a trip to your local bookstore. Consider the storylines of blockbuster movie releases. Or the content and themes of video games. What about children's literature, cartoons, games, or action figures? It fascinates me that the best-selling series of books in the Western world is a tale about witches and wizards. Billed as children's literature, Harry Potter and his magical adventures as a wizard in training at Hogwarts School of Witchcraft and Wizardry continue to mesmerize millions—enchanting kids and adults alike. Ancillary products such as trading cards, role-playing games, clothing, and even furniture have flooded the market. Of course, there is the blockbuster *Harry Potter* movie series (the seven films based on Rowling's Harry Potter books are scheduled to be released at the rate of one per year until 2007 and will no doubt receive much attention). Is it harmless fantasy or dangerous fascination? Is Harry's magic truly fictional or is it based on actual occultism? Does a Hollywood-Potter alliance foreshadow even darker and more powerful occult images?[2]

While some will draw stark comparison between the fantasy of Tolkien and Rowling, Tolkien's *Lord of the Rings*—a masterpiece tale about temptation to power with profound moral and religious implications in the enduring battle between good and evil—nevertheless revolves around sorcerers and magic. I wonder too about Pokémon with its "Energy Cards" that can make your Pokémon bigger and more powerful than some other Pokémon (like Abra and Kadabra, which are essentially psychic cards with magical powers). This too is supposedly kid stuff! Then there is the continuing appeal of angels, apparitions of Mary, and various kinds of miracles. New Age philosophy permeates the labels of teas, ginseng drinks, cosmetics, jewelry, study techniques, leadership principles, massage and meditation and relaxation, self-help—you name it!

The popularity of occultism in contemporary culture continues to grow at an alarming rate. Breeding a familiarity that blurs moral spiritual discernment, it expresses our society's not-so-subtle drift toward paganism. The various theological doctrines and overall worldview normally associated with occult practices are decidedly unbiblical. Some of it is in-your-face and some of it appears quite innocuous and subtle.

The lure of the occult and its associated forms has been an ongoing part of humanity's desperate search for meaning, power, help, and a glimpse into the future. Scripture tells us that Saul too came to the place where he went in search of a witch: "Find me a woman who can talk to the spirits of the dead," he commanded. "I'll go to her and find out what's going to happen" (1 Sam. 28:7, CEV). "There's a woman at Endor who can talk to spirits of the dead," his servants replied (verse 7, CEV).

Interestingly, Scripture tells us that earlier in his reign Saul had "removed from the land those who were mediums and spiritists" (verse 3, NASB). The land in view here was the "territory of Israel" (1 Sam. 27:1, NASB). In other words, forbidden agents of darkness had enchanted even God's own people. Saul was simply implementing the rather candid and strong warnings God had given Israel:

"Do not turn to mediums or spiritists; do not seek them out to be defiled by them. I am the Lord your God" (Lev. 19:31, NASB).

"A man or woman who is a medium or spiritist among you must be put to death. You are to stone them; their blood will be on their own heads" (Lev. 20:27, NIV).

"When you enter the land the Lord your God is giving you, do not learn to imitate the detestable ways of the nations there. Let no one be found among you who sacrifices his son or daughter in the fire, who practices divination or sorcery, interprets omens, engages in witchcraft, or casts spells, or who is a medium or spiritist or who consults the dead. Anyone who does these things is detestable to the Lord, and because of these detestable practices the Lord your God will drive out those nations before you. You must be blameless before the Lord your God. The nations you will dispossess listen to those who practice sorcery or divination. But as for you, the Lord your God has not permitted you to do so" (Deut. 18:9-14, NIV).

Why would God prohibit the many varied forms of occultism? First, divination is an extremely unreliable method of obtaining accurate information about the world, ourselves, others, and the future. Second, the various forms of occultism tend to pull people away from God. Third, the realm of the dead is not where individuals will find a way to living a joy-filled existence, nor will they find eternal life in the world of the departed (Isa. 8:19, 20). Fourth, sorcery and magic can unleash certain powers that are demonic in nature and as such are both spiritually deadly and no match for God's power (Ex. 7:11, 12, 22; 8:7, 18, 19). Fifth, harnessing either supernatural forces or the secret power of nature in order to influence events for one's own purposes is a direct affront to God's sovereignty and is the equivalent of making oneself into a god (one of the main tenets promoted in occultism is that humanity itself is a god). Finally, the various theological doctrines and overall worldview normally associated with occult practices are decidedly unbiblical. They teach such dangerous errors as the inherent divinity of all human beings, a denial of God's personal nature, and a rejection of what is holy, the reality of sin and human fallenness as well as any need for personal salvation.[3]

God had forbidden magic, fortune-telling, and contacting the dead, but here we find Saul searching for the Endor witch in a desperate attempt to contact the dead.[4] The author of Samuel purposely sandwiches this bizarre account in the middle of his story of how David's double life caught up with him during the destruction of Ziklag. Chapters 27, 29, and 30 of 1 Samuel report a dark time in David's life—one we would prefer to forget. It had almost drained his spiritual passion. Chapter 28, however, reports a strikingly dark time in Saul's life. At the very time David was strengthening himself in the Lord after 16 long months of moral compromise filled with deepening duplicity and continued failure, Saul was weakening himself further through the witch of Endor after years of spiritual apathy and purposeful disobedience. They were two men experiencing incredible distress (1 Sam. 28:5, 15; 30:6).[5] But they made diametrically opposed choices with radically different effects.

The story of Saul's visit to the Endor witch is not so much about the occult itself, or whether or not anyone can actually contact the dead, as it is about some of the reasons that people open themselves to it and what will happen in their lives when they do. This tragic incident provides insight into why some of us (and our own children) may become susceptible to its alluring power.

Why do people turn to the occult?

First, it attracts the spiritually empty, those to whom God is not already a living personal reality in their lives. Spiritual things are not real to them but are just ideas, theoretical concepts. When they do not have a God-dominated imagination, their imagination focuses elsewhere.

Three times the biblical author refers to Saul's spiritual emptiness. The first occasion simply tells us that "when Saul inquired of the Lord, the Lord did not answer him, either by dreams or by Urim or by prophets" (1 Sam. 28:6, NKJV). Later the king himself informs Samuel's assumed apparition that "God has departed from me and answers me no more, either through prophets or by dreams" (verse 15, NASB). Finally the apparition demands, "Why then do you ask me, since the Lord has departed from you and has become your adversary?" (verse 16, NASB).

When Saul sought God to learn the outcome of his pending battle with the Philistines, he received no answer. He then became like those just diagnosed with a terminal illness. Since regular medicine cannot heal, they grasp at any faint hope. If approved religion will not reassure, they go elsewhere. Should someone try Christianity and it doesn't seem to work or have any power or make any radical difference, it sets the stage for the entrance of another supernatural power and reality. It happens too when we don't see our Christian faith working in the lives of people around us. Dissatisfied or left unfulfilled and skeptical, we are unwittingly vulnerable to occultism in some form.

God's refusal to respond to Saul's pleas strikes a chord of concern in us. Why didn't the Lord answer him when the king inquired of Him before he sought a spiritist? Why is God silent at times? Isaiah 59:1-3 gives us one very valid explanation for God's silence, one that certainly applied to Saul at this time. Isaiah wrote: "your iniquities have separated you from your God; your sins have hidden his face from you, so that he will not hear" (Isa. 59:2, NIV). Remember, Saul continued in disobedience to God. He relentlessly sought the life of an innocent man and even attempted to spear his own son! Furthermore, he had the priests of the Lord slaughtered and approved of the destruction of an entire town. We've seen some regrets in him, but never any true yielding of the heart and turning from wickedness to righteousness. Isaiah does not say that God can't hear. Rather that He won't hear. It makes me stop and think about those moments in my life when God seems silent. Maybe He is waiting on me to confront and confess certain sins in my life.

Note that Saul had eliminated from his realm all common practices of religious manipulation, such as mediums and wizards. Outwardly he had conformed, but in the end his rigid orthodoxy did not help him. I find it interesting that he wound up doing the very thing he tried to suppress. We've done the very same from time to time. At first we felt convicted to get rid of something or to cease a certain practice, then when our regard for God began to shrink and our concern for our own desires began to grow, we were out the door hunting it down. The very thing we often try to get rid of will be the thing we turn to first in a moment of spiritual or moral emptiness.

Closely linked to spiritual emptiness is spiritual incongruity. I want you to notice that Saul demands what is forbidden. His story is one of contradictory behavior. He exterminates mediums, yet he seeks a medium himself. And when the woman refused to help, thinking it may be a trap, Saul swore to her by the Lord, saying, "As surely as the Lord lives, you will not be punished for this" (1 Sam. 28:10, NIV). Think about it! Saul's oath invoked the Lord to grant immunity to one who broke a divine command—Saul turned God against Himself.[6] It is just one more manifestation of the king's lifelong spiritual incongruities. His decision to go to Endor is just another expression of an inward inconsistency that characterized his whole life.[7] Saul is a divided self marked with shamed incongruity.[8] Whenever we are incongruent in our lives we open the door toward spiritual compromise with powers of darkness.

Second, people are more open to the occult when they do not have confidence in the Word of God or when they are satisfied with only partial obedience. The apparition reminds Saul that "as you did not obey the Lord and did not execute His fierce wrath on Amalek, so the Lord has done this thing to you this day" (verse 18, NASB). Years before Samuel had reprimanded the king for taking God's Word lightly and rendering only partial or selective obedience at best. "Has the Lord *as great* delight in burnt offerings and sacrifices," Samuel asks, "as in obeying the voice of the Lord? Behold, to obey is better than sacrifice, *and* to heed than the fat of rams. For rebellion *is as* the sin of witchcraft, and stubbornness *is as* iniquity and idolatry. Because you have rejected the word of the Lord, He also has rejected you from *being* king" (1 Sam. 15:22, 23, NKJV). Notice that Samuel compares Saul's disregard of the command of God with satanic sorcery. The king had manifested great zeal in suppressing idolatry and witchcraft, yet in his disobedience to the divine command he had been motivated by the same spirit of opposition to God and had been as much under the influence of Satan as are those who practice sorcery.[9] It was a rebellious spirit. "When one commences to travel in the path of rebellion, he yields himself to be controlled by an influence that is in opposition to the will of God. Satan controls the rebellious mind. Those who are thus controlled lose a calm trust in God, and have less and less disposition to yield loving obedience to His will. Satan becomes more and more familiar with them, until they seem to have no power to cease to rebel. In this respect, rebellion is as the sin of witchcraft."[10] First Samuel 28 has a play on the word to *hear*. Saul does not listen to the Lord, but he will listen to the witch of Endor!

Finally, many struggle with distress and restlessness and concern about what may be looming on the horizon.[11] Saul "was afraid, and his heart trembled greatly," Scripture tells us (1 Sam. 28:5, NKJV). The Philistines had gathered and set up camp at Shunem. The sight of their forces filled the king with dread. When the apparition asks, "Why have you disturbed me by bringing me up?" Saul tells it like it is: "I am greatly distressed; for the Philistines are waging war against me, and God has departed from me and answers me no more" (verse 15, NASB). All hope had fled his heart. Saul is simply a frantic man with no resources. When our world caves in on us and we are troubled or afraid or feeling alone, we are most vulnerable to impressions to reach out toward the occult, especially when we are already running on empty spiritually.

Brueggemann puts it well: "His [Saul's] decision to seek help from a medium is a measure of his moral exhaustion, his despairing faith, his failed life."[12]

## Joining the Dead

They say that in spite of sequels, imitations, and decades of horror flicks, one of the most terrifying movies ever made was George Romero's 1968 horror film *Night of the Living Dead*. It is a grisly tale of ghouls who rise from the grave and devour the living. The film reportedly has a grainy look, cheesy acting, and a preposterous premise. But the characters whom viewers intuitively root for are the ones who get eliminated with grisly dispatch. The claustrophobic tension mounts so ruthlessly that many early filmgoers had to leave the theater in the middle of the film.[13]

The title *Living Dead* is a contradiction, an oxymoron. But I think it aptly illustrates what happens when we make ourselves vulnerable to the occult. The powers of darkness devour the living. In the process we become *living dead*.

Saul's search for the Endor witch is the story of a man dying from the inside out.[14] It is a tale of endings, not beginnings, about death, not life. Saul, while very much alive (physically), is fast heading for destruction (spiritually, morally, emotionally, and finally physically). The voice purporting to be Samuel speaks only death, destruction, nullification.

The desperate king's response is one of piteous dread. He falls to the ground prostrate, powerless, his nobility stripped away (verse 20). The supposed connection with supernatural powers actually weakens Saul rather than strengthens him. It is an interesting existential phenomenon.

First, self becomes divided and loses identity. Scripture tells us that "Saul disguised himself by putting on other clothes, and went . . . to the woman by night" (verse 8, NASB). Going to Endor, by the way, meant crossing over enemy lines. Endor was about six miles away and two miles northeast of the Philistine camp. Anyway, the absence of royal clothing and jewelry insulated him from scrutiny by Philistine soldiers patrolling the roads in the area and shielded his true identity. I find it interesting that Scripture says he put on other clothes. Clothes in biblical imagery represented the person: their status, who they were, their character. Thus Saul became someone and something else. He goes to the medium not wanting to appear as his true royal self.[15]

Second, Saul experiences further spiritual, moral, and emotional weakening. When we search for the witches and their magic it leaves us more empty than before. Again, the supposed connection with supernatural powers enfeebles us rather than strengthens us.

Third, our quest for peace eludes us as our inner turmoil, distress, and fear only increase. Saul begins and ends the episode in fear. He is fearful at the beginning and terrified at the end, falling down like a dead man.

Fourth, we have a debilitating influence on the lives of others. While Saul's present sin was private and concealed in darkness, its consequences would soon become public and massive. The Lord would before long hand him and Israel over to the Philistines (verse 19). The king's failure affected others. *Patriarchs and Prophets* tells us that "by consulting that spirit of darkness Saul had destroyed himself. Oppressed by the horror of despair, it would be impossible for him to inspire his army with courage. Separated from the Source of strength, he could not lead the minds of Israel to look to God as their helper. Thus the prediction of evil would work its own accomplishment."[16]

Ultimately, dabbling with the occult results in physical death and eternal oblivion. "Tomorrow you and your sons will be with me," the being tells Saul (verse 19, NIV). In other words, to speak to the dead is to join the dead.[17] The futility of conjuring up the dead is that it brings only an announcement of death.[18] By consulting the dead Saul has merely given himself a preview of his own impending fate. As a result, the death pall descends on his distraught figure, even though physical life still remains.[19] It is a night of the living dead.

### Samuel One Last Time?

We have to stop and ask, Was it really Samuel? Brueggemann correctly warns: "Its vibrant narrative details have the potential of seducing us in our interpretation. The matter of summoning ghosts is an act sure to fascinate the religiously curious. A theological interpretation, however, must hold to a steady discipline against such fascination. The narrative has no real interest in the summoning of spirits or in the role or capacity of the woman."[20] We need to be careful what kind of and how much application we draw from this lesson about the dearly departed. But clearly we cannot conclude from this encounter that our loved ones can ask God to let us appear to them after we're dead, or that it's OK for us to seek to talk to the dead.

Scripture affirms the existence of a larger world of supernatural beings. In the Old Testament supernatural beings could manifest themselves in human form, but the other way around is not possible—human beings could not appear as superhuman.[21] *Patriarchs and Prophets* tells us that "it was not God's holy prophet that came forth at the spell of a sorcerer's incantation. Samuel was not present in that haunt of evil spirits. That supernatural appearance was produced solely by the power of Satan. He could as easily assume the form of Samuel as he could assume that of an angel of light, when he tempted Christ in the wilderness."[22] The Bible teaches that death is a sleep—the dead know not a thing!

Furthermore, "the message itself is sufficient evidence of its origin. Its object was not to lead Saul to repentance, but to urge him on to ruin; and this is not the work of God, but of Satan. Furthermore, the act of Saul in consulting a sorceress is cited in Scripture as one reason why he was rejected by God and abandoned to destruction: 'Saul died for his transgression which he committed against the Lord, even against the word of the Lord, which he kept not, and also for asking counsel of one that had a familiar spirit, *to inquire of it;* and inquired not of the Lord: therefore he slew him, and turned the kingdom unto David the son of Jesse' (1 Chron. 10:13, 14). Here it is distinctly stated that Saul inquired of the familiar spirit, not of the Lord. He did not communicate with Samuel, the prophet of God; but through the sorceress he held intercourse with Satan. Satan could not present the real Samuel, but he did present a counterfeit, that served his purpose of deception."[23]

### If With Your Heart

What does all this have to do with David? And spiritual passion?

At the very time David was strengthening himself in the Lord after 16 long months of compromise, duplicity, and failure, Saul was weakening himself further through the witch of Endor after years of spiritual apathy and purposeful disobedience. Two men experiencing incredible distress, they made diametrically opposed choices. Choices that had two radically different effects and eternal destinies. It reminds me of the words of Jeremiah: "You will seek Me and find *Me* when you search for Me with all your heart" (Jer. 29:13, NASB).

On the one hand, Scripture tells us that Saul sought the Lord (1 Sam. 28:6). But on the other hand, the Bible declares that he didn't (1 Chron. 10:13, 14). Scripture is blunt: "When Saul inquired of the Lord, the Lord did not answer him" (1 Sam. 28:6, NKJV). "Saul died because he was un-faithful to the Lord; he did not keep the word of the Lord and even consulted a medium for guidance, and did not inquire of the Lord. So the Lord put him to death and turned the kingdom over to David son of Jesse" (1 Chron. 10:13, 14, NIV). Ellen White reminds us that "God had borne long with Saul; and although his rebellion and obstinacy had well-nigh silenced the divine voice in the soul, *there was still opportunity for repentance.* But when in his peril he turned from God to obtain light from a confederate of Satan, he had cut the last tie that bound him to his Maker; he had placed himself fully under the control of that demoniac power which for years had been exercised upon him, and which had brought him to the verge of destruction."[24]

"The Lord never turned away a soul that came to Him in sincerity and humility. Why did He turn Saul away unanswered? The king had by his own act forfeited the benefits of all the methods of inquiring of God. He had rejected the counsel of Samuel the prophet; he had exiled David, the chosen of God; he had slain the priests of the Lord. Could he expect to be answered by God when he had cut off the channels of communication that Heaven had ordained? He had sinned away the Spirit of grace, and could he be answered by dreams and revelations from the Lord? Saul did not turn to God with humility and repentance. It was not pardon for sin and reconciliation with God, that he sought, but deliverance from his foes. By his own stubbornness and rebellion he had cut himself off from God. There could be no return but by the way of penitence and contrition; but the proud monarch, in his anguish and despair, determined to seek help from another source."[25]

Until to this bizarre event Saul could still have turned to the Lord.

Opportunity for repentance still existed. But the king had so rejected the will of God for him that when he sought God's help he could not find it. Saul did not at any time fully repent of his sin and turn from it. Although he had longed for help and guidance, he had persisted in doing things his own way, resisting the holy influence of the Spirit of God.

On the other hand, David not only turned *away* from his sin; he turned his whole life *to* God again and again. He kept coming back to God. That is the secret of spiritual passion, passion for God—a repentant and surrendered heart. Letting God be God in your life. "The Lord in His great mercy did not punish this error of His servant by leaving him to himself in his distress and perplexity; for though David, losing his grasp on divine power, had faltered and turned aside from the path of strict integrity, *it was still the purpose of his heart to be true to God.* While Satan and his host were busy helping the adversaries of God and of Israel to plan against a king who had forsaken God, the angels of the Lord were working to deliver David from the peril into which he had fallen."[26]

I like that, don't you? "It was still the purpose of his heart to be true to God." The intent of the heart—that's what passion is all about. What is the purpose of your heart? And mine? Sometimes we find the answer to that in how we relate to the subtle (and not so subtle) pagan influences surrounding us—music, various paraphernalia, videos and movies, books, games, even artwork. Sometimes we need to empty the closet, clear the mind, restrict our associations, change what we see or hear—and seek God fully. The promise will ever be there: "You will seek Me and find *Me* when you search for Me with all your heart" (Jer. 29:13, NASB).

"A final word: Be strong with the Lord's mighty power. Put on all of God's armor so that you will be able to stand firm against all strategies and tricks of the Devil. For we are not fighting against people made of flesh and blood, but against the evil rulers and authorities of the unseen world, against those mighty powers of darkness who rule this world, and against wicked spirits in the heavenly realms. Use every piece of God's armor to resist the enemy in the time of evil, so that after the battle you will still be standing firm. Stand your ground, putting on the sturdy belt of truth and the body armor of God's righteousness. For shoes, put on the peace that comes from the Good News, so that you will be fully prepared. In every battle you will need faith as your shield to stop the fiery arrows aimed at you by Satan. Put on salvation as your helmet, and take the sword of the Spirit, which is the word of God. Pray at all times and on every occasion in the power of the Holy Spirit. Stay alert and be persistent in your prayers" (Eph. 6:10-18, NLT).

---

[1] Richard Corliss, "Blair Witch Craft," *Time*, Aug. 16, 1999, pp. 57-64; John Leland, "The Blair Witch Cult," *Newsweek*, Aug. 16, 1999, pp. 44-49; Seth Stevenson, "In Search of the Blair Witch," *Newsweek*, Aug. 16, 1999, p. 47; Melissa August, "Welcome to Burkittsville," *Time*, Aug. 16, 1999, p. 62.

[2] See Richard Abanes, *Harry Potter and the Bible: The Menace Behind the Magic* (Camp Hill, Pa.: Horizon Books, 2001).

[3] Abanes, pp. 195-200.

[4] Technically speaking, she's not a witch. Witches practice magic and attempt to influence the future rather than just divine it. The witch of Endor is more properly a medium or a necromancer (one who divines by contacting the dead). Scripture calls her a *ba 'alat 'ob*, which denotes either one who owns and operates a necromatic pit, or one who controls a spirit (Cheryl Anne Brown, *No Longer Be Silent: First Century Jewish Portraits of Biblical Women* [Louisville: Westminster/John Knox Press, 1992], p. 206).

[5] Scripture portrays both David and Saul as persons caught up in deep crises. The author uses the same language for both: David is "greatly distressed" (1 Sam. 30:6); Saul is "deeply distressed" (1 Sam. 28:15, NKJV). The Hebrew literally means "in a very tight place." "Saul is in great distress and does not know what to do. In this instance he is similar to David in distress but different in the response. David does and succeeds; Saul does and fails" (Peter D. Miscall, *1 Samuel: A Literary Reading*, p. 168).

[6] Robert D. Bergen, *1, 2 Samuel*, p. 266.

[7] Dorothee Solle et al., *Great Women of the Bible in Art and Literature* (Grand Rapids: William B. Eerdmans Pub. Co., 1994), p. 179.

[8] Walter Brueggemann, *First and Second Samuel*, p. 193.

[9] Ellen G. White, *Patriarchs and Prophets*, p. 635.

[10] White, *The Spirit of Prophecy* (Battle Creek, Mich.: Seventh-day Adventist Pub. Assn., 1870), vol. 1, p. 365. "Rebellion originated with Satan, and all rebellion against God is directly due to satanic influence. Those who set themselves against the government of God have entered into an alliance with the archapostate, and he will exercise his power and cunning to captivate the senses and mislead the understanding. He will cause everything to appear in a false light. Like our first parents, those who are under his bewitching spell see only the great benefits to be received by transgression" (White, *Patriarchs and Prophets*, p. 635).

[11] Other of types of individuals consistently interested in occult phenomena include *the curious* (who experiment with demonic forces and/or magic without having a fully formed system of religious beliefs); *the bereaved* (whose grief incline them toward anything that offers knowledge of the dead); and *the psychically inclined* (who want to develop suspected latent powers). Here we focus on the types of individuals consistent with Saul's experience.

[12] Brueggemann, p. 193.

[13] Richard Zoglin, "They Came From Beyond," *Time*, Aug. 16, 1999, p. 64.

[14] Brueggemann, p. 192.

[15] *Ibid.*, p. 193.

[16] White, *Patriarchs and Prophets*, p. 681.

[17] Miscall, p. 172.

[18] *Ibid.*
[19] Robert P. Gordon, *I and II Samuel,* p. 192.
[20] Brueggemann, p. 196.
[21] Alden Thompson, *Samuel: From the Danger of Chaos to the Danger of Power,* p. 174.
[22] White, *Patriarchs and Prophets,* p. 679.
[23] *Ibid.,* p. 683.
[24] *Ibid.,* p. 679. (Italics supplied.)
[25] *Ibid.,* p. 676.
[26] *Ibid.,* p. 690. (Italics supplied.)

12

# GOOD GRIEF! THE SONG OF THE BOW

## I Samuel 31; 2 Samuel I

About the year A.D. 350, during the Iron Age in northern Europe, a ship carrying 40 or so warriors came ashore on a beach in what is now southern Denmark. With its open hull, overlapping planks, herringbone array of oars, and tall, matching bow and stern, the oak vessel embodied a classic Scandinavian form. The bearded warriors carried iron swords and wore woolen clothing. A modern observer would likely have assumed that they were Vikings—but the rampages of the Vikings would not begin for another 450 years. . . .

"When their ship's keel bit into the sand, the warriors hopped over the gunwales into the icy water. As a numbing rain slanted out of the bone-colored sky, they dragged their five-ton ship onto the beach, then marched into the woods, and after a time came upon a quiet village near a lake. A dozen thatch-roofed longhouses sheltered families with their livestock. Smokehouses, a blacksmith's forge, and other small buildings filled out the settlement.

"When the warriors attacked, young men scrambled outside, ready for the fight. The intruders, outnumbered, soon perished at the hands of the locals.

"The victors trudged off in the direction their attackers had come from and eventually found the empty ship. The next day they rigged horses to the vessel and hauled it inland to their lake. Once there, the men set about smashing the belongings collected from the bodies of the warriors: swords, lances, axes, and personal effects like coins, lockets, even tweezers and fingernail cleaners. The villagers fractured wooden spears and ax handles, splintered arrow shafts, and bent the arrowheads. The blacksmith took the swords, each as valuable as a horse, bent them into tortured shapes, and hurled them into the lake. . . .

"Someone hacked open the hull. As water gushed in, the villagers nudged the ship away from the bank and chanted prayers to the gods of the tribe. They slaughtered some horses and threw them into the water. Then they watched the ship heel over and slip beneath the surface."[1] The villagers believed that sacrificing such treasures would express gratitude for their victory to the gods believed to inhabit the lake.

Lakes were the churches—the sacred places—of many Iron Age peoples. The valuables deposited in the lakes of Denmark, as well as in Germany and England, suggest deeply held religious beliefs. Today archaeologists are retrieving fragments of this ship sacrifice from Nydam, a Danish bog the size of a baseball diamond in southern Denmark. As he supervises the excavations and ponders the incredible wealth preserved intact for nearly 17 centuries, archaeologist Peter Vang Petersen, asks, "What are the powers that make people destroy wealth in such amounts? These things we've found are very expensive. To an Iron Age man a sword cost as much as a modest car today. It was a sign of prestige."[2]

It amazes us today that someone would drag an enemy ship inland to a sacred lake and scuttle it with its valuables just to thank the gods for success in war. But the idea of such sacrifice is an ancient and widespread concept.

When the Philistines discovered Saul's body the day following Israel's ill-fated battle with them at Gilboa, their mockery and celebration began in earnest. The finding of the dead king's body explained why the Israelites had fled so quickly. Scripture tells us that the Philistines beheaded Saul and hauled his severed head and weapons from place to place "throughout the land of the Philistines to carry the good news to the houses of their idols and to the people" (1 Sam. 31:9, NRSV).[3] Notice that the triumphal display included the houses of their idols. Eventually Saul's weapons wound up in the temple of Ashtaroth (verse 10). Interestingly, the New Revised Standard Version reading—"good news"—reflects the word "gospel" employed in the Greek Septuagint. Ironically, it is also the same Greek word for "gospel" used in the story of Jesus.[4] Even the Hebrew counterpart means to "bear good tidings." In other words, the Philistines share the "gospel"—the good news of victory—with their people. In the process, they are praising their gods.

In addition, the invaders sent the naked, decapitated bodies of Saul and his three sons a few miles east to Beth-shean, where they had them hung on a wall for further shame and insult as they rotted in the sun, grew maggots, and were picked apart by birds. By doing so, the Philistines were making a religious claim—their gods had won. The death of an enemy king was always good news. Strategically, it meant that the military threat had lost its main force. Theologically, it indicated that the enemy god had gone down to defeat, for when the king perished, the ruler's god had failed.[5] The military and the political were linked to the religious. Ultimately God was the one humiliated in the mocking of Saul.

While the majority of Israelites in the region reacted to the Philistine victory with fear and flight, the people of Jabesh-gilead displayed incredible boldness and character. "Now when the inhabitants of Jabesh-gilead heard what the Philistines had done to Saul, all the valiant men rose and walked all night, and took the body of Saul and the bodies of his sons from the wall of Beth-shan, and they came to Jabesh and burned them there. They took their bones and buried them under the tamarisk tree at Jabesh, and fasted seven days" (verses 11-13, NASB).

The people of Jabesh-gilead remembered Saul as he had once been: a savior, deliverer, someone larger than life, willing to risk himself on their behalf (1 Sam. 11:1-11). Years earlier, when Nahash the Ammonite had besieged their small town, they wanted to arrange a deal: "'Make a treaty with us, and we will be your servants,' they pleaded.

"'All right,'" Nahash said, 'but only on one condition. I will gouge out the right eye of every one of you as a disgrace to all Israel!'" (verses 1, 2, NLT). When Saul heard about their plight the Holy Spirit filled him. Within hours he began assembling an army. Through God's power Saul's passionate response saved the people of Jabesh-gilead and routed the enemy. Now they came with resolve (and perhaps some risk). The trek was difficult and dangerous, especially at night, since Beth-shean was about 15 miles away, and one had to ford the Jordan River and enter Philistine-held territory to get there. But they were not afraid to be identified with the dead king. Taking the body, they rescued it from humiliation as well as the memory of Saul from shame. They remembered his fidelity and the way he had changed their life and their future, and now they responded in kind. Thus 1 Samuel "closes with an act that is not a power play, a calculated show of restraint, a deception, or an attempt to buy someone's loyalty; it closes with pathos, with a memory of Saul's finest hour."[6] May we accept and imitate their example. May our memories of kindness be long and of offenses be short. It's never too late to say thanks.

### When Your Enemy Falls

It took nearly four days before David learned what had happened to Saul.[7] Apparently he heard of it on his third day back in Ziklag after routing the Amalekite marauders who had sacked his home and kidnapped his family (2 Sam. 1:1, 2). As he and his men labored to restore their ruined homes, they waited with anxious hearts for tidings of the battle which they knew must have taken place between Israel and the Philistines.[8] Suddenly a young man rushed breathless into the camp, his clothes torn and dust on his head. He made straight for David and fell to the ground at his feet. David could tell from his appearance that one of the armies had suffered tragic defeat. But which? Was it Achish and the Philistines or Saul and the Israelites? In a moment more, the young man gave his report, each word stabbing David to the heart. Israel had fled before her enemies. Large numbers had fallen on the battlefield. Saul and Jonathan were dead (verse 4).

"How do you know that Saul and Jonathan are dead?" David asked, not wanting to accept the tragic news just at face value, hoping, perhaps, that the tale wasn't true.

"I happened to be on Mount Gilboa," the young man replied, "and I saw that Saul was leaning on his spear and that the chariots and cavalry of the enemy were closing in on him. Then he turned around, saw me, and called to me. I answered, 'Yes, sir!' He asked who I was, and I told him that I was an Amalekite. Then he said, 'Come here and kill me! I have been badly wounded, and I'm about to die.' So I went up to him and killed him, because I knew that he would die anyway as soon as he fell.

Then I took the crown from his head and the bracelet from his arm, and I have brought them to you, sir" (verses 5-10, TEV).

No doubt the Amalekite expected David to reward him. "I took the crown from his head and the bracelet from his arm, and I have brought them to you, sir!" he said. Evidently supposing that David must certainly cherish resentment toward his relentless persecutor, this battlefield scavenger hoped to secure honor to himself as the slayer of the king. He confidently expected that David would hail the tidings with joy, and that he would receive a rich reward for his role.[9] After all, he had brought the symbols of royal legitimacy—crown and bracelet. Surely there was an open path now to the long-awaited throne, and David would now possess the royal insignia.

Those with David watched and waited to see how their leader would respond to the good news of Saul's death. It is a breathtaking moment in the story, one in which a lesser person might have rejoiced and thanked the bearer of good tidings. In that instant David knew that the cloud that had so long hung over his head had finally lifted and that the expectations of years were on the point of being realized. His fugitive years had ceased. The way was open for him to return home to Israel. The path to the throne was clear. The promises of God were coming to reality. Saul was dead, and he was not in any way implicated.

But David, however, was not a lesser person. He responded not in glee but in pathos. It was the king who was dead—the Lord's anointed. Instead of celebrating, he grieved. Having the unambiguous tokens of Saul's death—the royal crown and bracelet—in his possession, he was devastated by the reality of the royal family's destruction. Scripture tells us that, overwhelmed by heartache, "David took hold of his clothes and tore them, and so also did all the men who were with him. They mourned and wept and fasted until evening for Saul and his son Jonathan and for the people of the Lord and the house of Israel, because they had fallen by the sword" (verses 11, 12, NASB). It was uncalculated, spontaneous, profound, and heartfelt grief.

When David learned that his most determined enemy was dead, he did not rejoice. Rather, he spontaneously displayed his loyalty, his respect, and his admiration for his fallen antagonist.[10]

How do you respond when someone you have been in conflict with meets failure? When your enemy fails or falls and the way opens for your own personal success? How do you feel? What do you say or do? It is human nature to rejoice when an enemy gets into trouble. How about you?

During the Battle of Santiago on July 3, 1898, the battleship *Texas* swept past the burning Spanish ship *Vizcaya*. When his men began to cheer, Captain John Woodward Philip restrained them by saying, "Don't cheer. The poor devils are dying." Proverbs enunciates the timeless moral principle at play here: "Do not rejoice when your enemy falls, and do not let your heart be glad when he stumbles" (Prov. 24:17, NKJV).[11] "You will be punished if you take pleasure in someone's misfortune," the book adds (Prov. 17:5, TEV). The point is that "your glee may well be a more punishable sin than all the guilt of your enemy."[12] Such rejoicing might prompt the Lord to give relief to your enemy while He disciplines you for your sinful attitude. It is so easy to say "It serves them right!" and go on and crow inwardly or to our circle of friends. But when we do, the attitude we manifest becomes a decimating spiritual/moral cancer. Like one of those malicious e-mail viruses that once opened replicates itself exponentially to the place we are spiritually bankrupt.

Job understood the moral significance of the way we respond when someone we have been in conflict with stumbles or falls. When his friends called his character into question, Job declared, "I have never been glad when my enemies suffered, or pleased when they met with disaster. No, I would not allow my tongue to sin or invoke a curse against his life" (Job 31:29, 30, my paraphrase). The patriarch kept both heart and tongue sensitive to the life and feelings of his enemies. So did David. It's the stuff of spiritual passion.

David knew what it was like to be made fun of while down and out. "When I was in trouble," he writes, "they were all glad and gathered around to make fun of me. . . . Like men who would mock a cripple, they glared at me with hate. How much longer, Lord, will you just look on? Rescue me. . . . Don't let my enemies . . . gloat over my defeat. Don't let those who hate me for no reason smirk with delight over my sorrow" (Ps. 35:15-19, TEV). "To You, O Lord, I lift up my soul. O my God, I trust in You; let me not be ashamed; let not my enemies triumph over me" (Ps. 25:1, 2, NKJV).

Mocked when we're down is no fun! It hurts! The heart is crushed and self-worth and hope wither.

We're talking here about attitudes—how we view people. How sensitive are we to the feelings and hurts of others, even those we are in conflict with and who have hurt us deeply?

Ellen White writes that "David's grief at the death of Saul was sincere and deep, evincing the generosity of a noble nature. He did not exult in the fall of his enemy. The obstacle that had barred his access to the throne of Israel was removed, but at this he did not rejoice."[13]

It makes me wonder what kind of attitudes our children read from us in terms of people and their failures. Some of us humiliate people who have fallen, even when they are not our enemy! Are our inmost feelings or our words and actions contrary to the example of Jesus, who died for a world of enemies? We must show a love that grieves at the fate of those who go contrary to right or who may have offended us in some way (Eze. 33:11; Luke 19:41, 42). How we respond to the misfortunes of those who give us pain says a lot toward how much our heart is like God's. It speaks volumes about our spiritual passion.

### The Art of Lament

On November 22, 1963, an assassin's bullet killed President John Fitzgerald Kennedy as his motorcade wound through Dallas, Texas. It was a profound moment of both personal and national tragedy. Jacqueline lost her husband, and at age 34 faced raising two young children alone. The American people lost a popular young president who had energized their imagination about the nation's bright future. Camelot was gone forever. Our nation was in shock. Not only was our president dead; someone had murdered him. The outpouring of shame, anger, confusion, and grief was spontaneous and heartfelt. It was a humiliating and ignominious moment for America.

Sometime during those early moments of arranging Kennedy's funeral, Jacqueline refused to be pushed aside by those wanting to take over, and courageously planned the president's state funeral herself. Somehow she sensed that the requiem needed to be a sensitive blending of personal and national lament. Art and heart must flow together in a moving personal and national expression of extraordinary anguish, dignified celebration, and enduring resolve and hope. Both her family and her nation needed to unleash their grief, savor the moment of remembrance, and move on. That blending of art and heart included President Kennedy being carried on a horse-drawn caisson from the White House to the rotunda of the Capitol, where hundreds of thousands of people filed past the coffin of the slain leader. The state funeral included representatives from 92 nations. As many as 1 million people may have lined the streets of Washington as the funeral procession made its way slowly to Arlington National Cemetery. An eternal flame lit by his wife and brothers marked the grave.

Jacqueline's agony worked catalytically. Her pain created one of the most sensitive and moving expressions of mourning ever experienced by our nation. In the process she won the admiration of the world. Thereafter it seemed the public would never allow her the privacy she desired for herself and her children.

Scripture tells us that following that painful day of stunned grief and anguish over the death of Saul, David chanted a lament over Saul and Jonathan (2 Sam. 1:17):

> "Your beauty, O Israel, is slain on your high places!
> How have the mighty fallen!
> Tell it not in Gath,
> Proclaim it not in the streets of Ashkelon,
> Or the daughters of the Philistines will rejoice,
> The daughters of the uncircumcised will exult.
> O mountains of Gilboa,
> Let not dew or rain be on you, nor fields of offerings;
> For there the shield of the mighty was defiled,
> The shield of Saul, not anointed with oil.
> From the blood of the slain, from the fat of the mighty,
> The bow of Jonathan did not turn back,
> And the sword of Saul did not return empty.
> Saul and Jonathan, beloved and pleasant in their life,
> And in their death they were not parted;
> They were swifter than eagles,
> They were stronger than lions.

O daughters of Israel, weep over Saul,
> Who clothed you luxuriously in scarlet,
> Who put ornaments of gold on your apparel.
How have the mighty fallen in the midst of the battle!
> Jonathan is slain on your high places.
I am distressed for you, my brother Jonathan;
> You have been very pleasant to me.
> Your love to me was more wonderful
> Than the love of women.
How have the mighty fallen,
> And the weapons of war perished!"

—2 Samuel 1:19-27, NASB

In his lament David touches on the enormity of Israel's loss and presents a heartrending reminiscence of his friendship with Jonathan. The future king of Israel forgets all he suffered at the hands of Saul as he thinks only of the king's early manhood. Saul had hated David, pursued him, and made his life miserable. David had lived nearly 11 years on the run in a world controlled by Saul's hatred.

What God had done for Saul, though, far outweighed anything Israel's first king ever did to David. And that is what David chose to remember and deal with.[14] As with the men of Jabesh-gilead, death had obliterated the remembrance of Saul's distrust and cruelty. Now David thought of nothing in the former ruler's life but what was noble and kingly. He linked the name of Saul with that of Jonathan, whose friendship with David had been true and unselfish.[15] David includes a special stanza for Jonathan, his soul mate. The words of his lament suddenly turn from the refrain of the assembly to the grief of a single heart: "I grieve for you, Jonathan my brother." In his poem David called his friend's love "wonderful." He distinguished the sacrificial nature of this friendship from anything else that anyone had ever demonstrated to him. So determined was Jonathan that David be king, a position that he himself stood to inherit, that he committed his entire life to that end. David found that astonishing.

Titling his lament "Song of the Bow," he commanded, "Teach it to sons of Judah. Teach it to the people." And so it became part of the book of Jashar, a book of remembrance of significant Israelites and their deeds (verse 18).

David's personal pain created one of the most sensitive and moving expressions of mourning ever penned or uttered.[16] When Israel witnessed David in his grief, it saw him in his fullest, most faithful, most powerful form—passion for God at its best. His poem marked a deep, precious, and painful moment in the life of Israel.[17] It was a day of personal as well as national tragedy. His poetic lament nobly and honestly grieved both the personal and national tragedy. David sings of the splendor of Saul and Jonathan and the enormous loss Israel now faces. The present death is so devastating because the previous heroism and potential had been so evident. It is liberating grief that permits Israel to give full expression to this moment of extraordinary defeat. As Bruggemann writes: "Through the eloquence of David, Israel lingers in the loss, lingers without resolution or manipulation, lingers in the grief, unashamed."[18]

In the process we the reader also learn how to lament.[19] All too often we have no easy way to process our hurt. But this poem can be our model.[20] As it accepts the hurt and focuses on the positive it lances the soul's painful blister of grief. Israel needed to notice the hurt. She needed to embrace defeat and eventually move beyond her loss. It is the same with every generation, with every individual, family, or congregation at significant moments of loss, failure, defeat, or tragedy. The future king of Israel gave us the words and the permission to grieve and led the way.

David lamented because he cared and because he was willing and able to bring his total attention to the reality of death.[21] Life matters. And when it does we will lament its loss. Seventy percent of the psalms are laments. After all, David repeatedly endured loss and experienced disappointment. The prospect of death hovered over him continually. The death of those he loved or trusted was a painful reality. He neither avoided, denied, nor soft-pedaled any of those difficulties but faced everything. In the process he let his heart respond to it all.[22] It's the only way spiritual passion keeps its equilibrium.

Peterson correctly asserts that "a failure to lament is a failure to connect."[23] The failure to grieve loss raises barriers to newness.[24] Brueggemann notes that "death [or loss of any kind] has a way of permitting us to focus on the larger realities, to transcend the details of hurt and affront. . . . Grief has a way of focusing the picture, permitting in hyperbolic expression what is true and best remembered."[25] "Lament notices and attends, savors and delights—details, images, relationships. Pain entered into, accepted, and owned can become poetry. It's no less pain, but it's no longer ugly."[26]

When Katie told Kevin she wanted a separation, blaming him for her pain and disappointment, she brought up the abortions. They had had sex before they got married, and she had gotten pregnant—not once, but twice. She had had both pregnancies aborted. But Kevin couldn't understand what that had to do with their separation. Why was she bringing it up now when it had happened eight years ago?

One morning, about two weeks after their separation, the husband was praying. "Kevin," he heard God say, "you and Katie need to have a funeral! You need to ask her to forgive you." For a while they had talked about having a funeral after the abortions, but they never did. Over time it got lost in the pressures of life. Now Kevin decided to do it. He wasn't sure how Katie would react, but he called her and asked if she would be willing to go with him to a waterfall that held a special place in their journey together and have a funeral for their aborted babies. "Whatever our future holds," he told her, "we need to find closure on this." She seemed not only willing but eager.

They had always imagined that their lost babies had been a boy and a girl, so Kevin bought matching boy and girl baby dolls. He also bought a hatchet. He bought some things for a lunch and stowed everything in his backpack before picking up his wife.

When they pulled into the parking lot at the trail base the wind was screaming down the mountains. The sky had clouded up, and it was turning cold. Snow began to fall. Everything looked menacing. But despite the weather, it was a beautiful hike. Along the way they both quietly reminisced their painful journey together, their moral compromises, the abortions, the guilt and shame, their blaming each other, and their fear of rejection. Nearing the falls, they left the trail and found a level spot. Kevin opened his backpack, took out his Bible, a tarp, and the two dolls. Kneeling on the tarp, they prayed, asking God to be present. Then Kevin asked Katie to name the girl doll. She remembered a high school teacher named Shawn and named her doll Shawna. Then it was his turn. He remembered his feelings of rejection because his younger brother had been named after his dad, so he called the boy doll Kevin, after himself.

Katie wanted him to go first, so he held the boy doll in his arms and told him how sorry he was for having premarital sex with his mother. Beginning to cry, he found it hard to talk. Kevin said that since he was older and more spiritually mature he should have protected the baby's mother. He explained to the baby how sorry he was for his selfishness and not protecting it because he was so afraid of rejection. Then he told God that someday when He returned their babies to them he would ask them to forgive him, and then they would get to know their brother and sister and their grandparents.

Kevin and Katie confessed to both dolls and asked forgiveness. They read the promise of resurrection (1 Thess. 4:16, 17) to each other. It was freezing cold. The wind was still blowing fiercely, and fog had swept into the mountains around them. Because the ground was frozen, Kevin carefully buried the dolls under the tight, dense branches of a little gnarled alpine shrub where neither animals nor people could find or disturb them. The couple were crying and holding on to each other tightly as Kevin began praying. He asked God to forgive them for both abortions and to hold only him accountable, because he had finally come to understand that he should have been responsible for protecting Katie.

Suddenly the wind stopped blowing, and it was absolutely still. The clouds parted and the sun shone down on them, right where they were standing. It was as if God was putting His arms around them and saying, "You are forgiven!" Laughing and weeping together, they sensed they were standing on holy ground. And they felt so light and free—so cleansed and forgiven—as they walked back down to the falls in the sunshine. There at the falls, Kevin took the hatchet from his backpack. Holding it flat in his hands, he said, "I've been a slave to anger and bitterness toward you. I have harbored resentment and isolated myself from you. By the grace of God, I transfer all that anger and bitterness to this hatchet." Then he walked over to the edge and threw it into the water at the base of the falls. Freed from the pain of the past, they went on to build their lives together.[27]

Unresolved grief multiplies problems. But grief can become a catalyst for personal growth and spiritual breakthrough. For David and the nation of Israel, it both expressed spiritual passion and nurtured it within their interior world.

David's fugitive years thus close with profound personal and national tragedy. It is a moment that tests the integrity of his inner private world, calling forth his real feelings toward the failure of someone who has hurt him deeply. And it is a moment that tests his courage to openly acknowledge the hurt, embrace loss, savor the memories, and move beyond with resolve and hope. Both tests proved that in spite of 11 years of faith on the run he had never lost his passion for God.

[1] Michael Klesius, "Mystery Ships From a Danish Bog," *National Geographic*, May 2000, pp. 28-35.

[2] *Ibid.*

[3] One reading supports the idea that the Philistines dispatched messengers with the news of their great victory; another reading suggests that they sent Saul's head and weapons throughout their territory as brutal evidence of their victory. See Ralph W. Klein, *1 Samuel*, p. 289.

[4] Alden Thompson, *Samuel: From the Danger of Chaos to the Danger of Power*, p. 180.

[5] Walter Brueggemann, *First and Second Samuel*, pp. 208, 209.

[6] Peter D. Miscall, *1 Samuel: A Literary Reading*, p. 182.

[7] See table of suggested order of events in Robert D. Bergen, *1, 2 Samuel*, p. 285.

[8] Ellen G. White, *Patriarchs and Prophets*, pp. 694, 695.

[9] *Ibid.*, p. 695.

[10] Bergen, p. 284.

[11] Here we are told not to rejoice or gloat over the misfortune of our enemies. How do we reconcile this passage with other portions of Scripture that celebrate God's triumph over enemies (Ex. 15; Ps. 136:10, 17-22)? "The difference is attitude; diligently resolving to praise God for His victory rather than the defeat of our enemies" (see Robert L. Alden, *Proverbs: A Commentary on an Ancient Book of Timeless Advice* [Grand Rapids: Baker Book House, 1983], p. 174).

[12] Derek Kidner, *The Proverbs* (Downers Grove, Ill.: InterVarsity Press, 1978), p. 155.

[13] White, *Patriarchs and Prophets*, pp. 695, 696.

[14] Eugene Peterson, *Leap Over a Wall*, p. 116.

[15] White, *Patriarchs and Prophets*, pp. 695, 696.

[16] Bergen, p. 290.

[17] Bruggemann, p. 214.

[18] *Ibid.*

[19] Peterson, p. 120.

[20] Brueggemann, p. 218.

[21] Peterson, p. 115.

[22] *Ibid.*

[23] *Ibid.*, p. 121.

[24] Brueggemann, p. 214.

[25] *Ibid.*, p. 216.

[26] Peterson, p. 119.

[27] Kevin Campbell as told by Carrol Grady, "Two Dolls and a Hatchet," *Adventist Review*, Feb. 17, 2000, pp. 8-11.

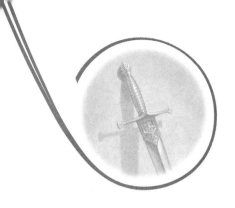

Epilogue

# WHAT YOU HEAR IN THE DARK

The incident happened in an instant, almost too fast to be noticed. It was a real feat of dodging, quick stops, leaps, and running for life. But the squirrel made it, unscathed and alive!

It had been in a ditch alongside the road when the sound of approaching cars spooked it. As it leaped up from the ditch to dash to its home across the road, it darted in front of two vehicles hurtling in opposite directions.

Now, I've seen the narrow escapes of squirrels darting across the road before, but none as dramatic as this one. This quick-witted squirrel narrowly evaded eight wheels rolling at 50-plus miles per hour. It had nearly made it to the middle of the road when the first car overran it. Hitting the brakes before being crushed by a front wheel, it spun around to race back. By now the car was fully overhead and an oncoming rear wheel threatened the squirrel's exit. Braking yet again, it spun around a second time. It ran out from beneath the car on the opposite side barely an instant before the other rear wheel grabbed its tail.

That's when it met the second car. One of the car's front wheels nearly got it. In the split second this car was over it, it again spun around. As with the first car, an oncoming rear wheel now threatened its exit. One more frantic U-turn and a final a hair-raising sprint from beneath the car thrust the squirrel out the opposite side to freedom—skirting one last menacing rear wheel.

It had happened so fast, but it had made it—unscathed! Turning to my son, who was riding in the car with me, I gasped, "Did you see that!"

"Yeah, Dad! Awesome. That's one lucky squirrel!"

In his roller-coaster experience of running for his life through 11 fugitive years David almost didn't make it. The twists and turns, intrigue, and close calls and narrow escapes threatened his life physically, emotionally, spiritually, and morally. Leaving him emotionally breathless, the experience stretched his spiritual passion to the limit. "God," David voiced at one point in the bizarre and wearying pursuit, "I am running to you for dear life; the chase is wild" (Ps. 7:1, Message).

The chase had indeed been wild. The biblical story of that relentless pursuit has kept us reading and wondering what would come next. Would David make it not just with his life, but with his heart? When it would be all over, would the fugitive still have *a heart like His?* Would his passion for God hold out? As he comes out the other end of his fugitive years physically alive, with dignity and grace and spiritual passion very much intact— even deepened—we're impressed if not awed. He's one lucky guy! Deep inside, we ponder whether we'd have made it. Do I have that kind of staying power? that kind of passion? And where did David get it?

His fugitive years have taught us something about human nature. Even more, it has revealed something about ourselves—our motives, our values, our responses. Most important, we have discovered something about spiritual passion. What it takes. The threats it faces and how it endures. And through it all, we have especially grasped something about God!

The story of David is an account of overwhelming passion for God. His strongest instinct was to relate his life to God. In comparison, nothing else seemed to matter at all.[1] He opened his heart to God, loved God, believed God, thought about God, imagined God, addressed God, prayed to God, sang to God, and obeyed God. David framed his whole world around God. The intense pressures and unrelenting trials of David's fugitive years, though, had threatened to diminish his passion for God. The conditions and experiences of life that can affect spiritual passion are real.[2] They can jade or sap it. David's 11 anxiety-filled fugitive years sorely tested him. It was one of the deepest, longest, and darkest valleys of his entire life. Something he had never ever experienced. As we have followed him into that valley we have discovered how he both blew it and yet grew. We learned how fear, jealousy, pride, envy, lack of faith, a competitive spirit, anger, lying, and other mental-attitude sins (both on our own part or by others) can overcome us.

As with David, our inner personal world can absorb just so much. Although we could reason that we should be ready to take it all in and cope with ease, we all too often aren't so prepared. David's fugitive years highlight some of the issues that slowly drain off zeal and threaten to leave us with loss of heart. In the future king's experiences we can see reflected our own relationship with God and the dangers that we may face. We catch a glimpse too of faith on the run—faith that must play itself out in the realities of day-to-day life. Perhaps it is faith challenged and buffeted and perhaps retreating because some things may be too much for us. Or it may be faith required to respond immediately with hardly an instant to weigh options or motives or determine right from wrong in situations that offer us no apparent hope or help.

Again, as with David struggling through his fugitive years, our faith is often on the run, working itself out in the nitty-gritty of life with hardly a moment to breathe. Sometimes our faith is in retreat, challenged with almost overwhelming failure or constant pressure that wearies spiritual passion—but always on the run, whether forward or backward, because a life of passion for God is never static. It keeps moving because the circumstances and experiences of life around us—our life—never stand still. We can never claim that we have arrived, but then neither can we ever say that we have failed for good.

It is here that I find myself plummeting with David into some of the darkest areas of my own inner life—into the very depths of my own sinful nature. Countless things about David can inspire us toward the most noble human emotions and behavior. I see so many things in him I wish I had, but here, in his fugitive years, I come face to face with some things I'm scared that I really do have. His experience touches my most guarded yearnings deep within the interior of my soul. As my imagination draws me into the drama of these 11 years I am stirred, shocked, amazed, and forced to think a few hard thoughts about myself. What about pride? jealousy? my ambitions or integrity? How do I handle anger and dashed hopes? How do I relate to the failure or defeat of my enemy? unrelenting pressure? the emotionally draining chaos? And what about my grip on God? When the going gets rough, do I go it alone or lean on God? I cannot journey through David's fugitive years without my interior world of motives and feelings and ambitions and values and responses coming into focus. Am I ready for what I see? Am I willing to let God show me what I am unable to recognize on my own? Here I learn, too, that when incessantly pressed to the point of breaking, we can come to the place where we doubt both God's motives and His actions. It can then lead to compromise and independent behavior. Is that possible with me?

"Genuine conversion brings us daily into communion with God," Ellen White writes. "There will be temptations to meet, and a strong undercurrent drawing us from God to our former state of indifference and sinful forgetfulness of God. No human heart can remain strong without divine grace. No man can remain converted unless he takes care of himself and the Master has a care for him. Unless the heart holds fast to God, and God holds fast to him, he will become self-confident and exalted and will surely stumble and fall."[3] "He who strives to serve God will encounter a strong undercurrent of wrong. His heart needs to be barricaded by constant watchfulness and prayer, or else the embankment will give way; and like a millstream, the undercurrent of wrong will sweep away the safeguard. No renewed heart can be kept in a condition of sweetness without the daily application of the salt of the Word. Divine grace must be received daily, or no man will stay converted."[4] David's fugitive years are a sobering reminder of such things.

It's hard to keep perspective when our faith is on the run. But David's fugitive years can give us some bearings and point out potential traps. They tell us the kind of things to expect. Knowing some of them enables our faith to run well and our passion for God to endure. We can also learn to trust God in a new way! In the process we can become a different man or woman, wholehearted and passionate for God. That's what I want—to be ever passionate for Him no matter what life may bring.

The story of David, though, is more about God than the human being. Its purpose is to reveal Him to us—to show us what He is like and what He has done. Through David God opens to us something about Himself. *Faith on the run*—retreating, advancing? What does that tell us about God?

Why would He ever be worthy of such passion? How does faith on the run answer that one?

Remember Chambers' reading on Matthew 10:27?—"What I tell you in darkness, that speak ye in the light:" "At times God puts us through the discipline of darkness to teach us to heed Him. Song birds are taught to sing in the dark, and we are put into the shadow of God's hand until we learn to hear Him. 'What I tell you in darkness'—watch where God puts you into darkness, and when you are there keep your mouth shut. . . . When you are in the dark, listen, and God will give you a very precious message for someone else when you get into the light."[5]

We must learn to hear in the dark so that we will have something profound to say about God in the light! Spiritual passion and the dark are linked. Faith on the run will always teach us about God—if we listen. Like David and the songbirds, we'll have something to sing from our darkness. What will that song about God be?

Psalm 18 gives us a glimpse of what David learned from the dark about God. He penned it when the Lord finally delivered him from the wild chase of his fugitive years (and some testy moments as Israel's king). In a rush of metaphors David relives his narrow escapes and unexpected victories, probing into their meaning. As he recounts the story of God's gracious dealings in the past his words pile up staccato-style, expressing the nature of God as David experienced Him in the darkness. God was deliverer. Shield. Safe retreat. Cliff. Stronghold and rock.

David's magnificent hymn of praise begins with a profoundly personal statement: "I love you." The verb is unusual, but indicates an intimacy in his relationship with God reflected throughout the psalm. It becomes clear as the psalm progresses that such intimacy arose from an awareness of God's companionship in a series of dangerous and mortal crises.[6] When faith was on the run and passion put to the stretch, God was there to be known—intimately. No psalm gathers more of his life together in one place than does this one.[7] Listen:

> "I love you, O Lord, my strength.
> The Lord is my rock, my fortress and my deliverer;
> > my God is my rock, in whom I take refuge.
> He is my shield and the horn of my salvation, my stronghold.
> > I call to the Lord, who is worthy of praise,

and I am saved from my enemies.
The cords of death entangled me;
    the torrents of destruction overwhelmed me.
The cords of the grave coiled around me;
    the snares of death confronted me.
In my distress I called to the Lord;
    I cried to my God for help.
From his temple he heard my voice;
    my cry came before him, into his ears. . . .
He brought me out into a spacious place;
    he rescued me because he delighted in me."

—Psalm 18:1-19, NIV

David presents his thoughts through poetical language borrowed from the scenes of the Red Sea in Sinai (verses 7-20). And yet the sheer volume of God's gracious help in his life did warrant a comparison with Israel's deliverance from Egypt. We too have our Red Seas. And God will do as much for us as He did for David. "My cry came before Him!" David writes. The voice is thin and solitary, but the answer shakes creation.[8] Can you imagine a God like that when your faith is on the run? How could you not have passion for Him!

So full is David's vision of God from his dark experience of fugitive life that he finishes with a resounding doxology:

"The Lord lives! Praise be to my Rock!
Exalted be God my Savior!
He is the God who avenges me,
    who subdues nations under me,
    who saves me from my enemies.
You exalted me above my foes;
    from violent men you rescued me.
Therefore I will praise you among the nations, O Lord;
I will sing praises to your name.
    He gives his king great victories;
    he shows unfailing kindness to his anointed,
to David and his descendants forever."

—Verses 46-50, NIV

In the middle of these profound thoughts about God David voices a few things about himself. Things that at first seem out of place:

"The Lord has dealt with me according to my righteousness;
 according to the cleanness of my hands he has rewarded me.
For I have kept the ways of the Lord;
 I have not done evil by turning from my God.
All his laws are before me;
 I have not turned away from his decrees.
I have been blameless before him and have kept myself from sin.
The Lord has rewarded me according to my righteousness,
 according to the cleanness of my hands in his sight.
To the faithful you show yourself faithful,
 to the blameless you show yourself blameless,
 to the pure you show yourself pure,
 but to the crooked you show yourself shrewd.
You save the humble but bring low those whose eyes are haughty.
You, O Lord, keep my lamp burning;
 my God turns my darkness into light.
With your help I can advance against a troop;
 with my God I can scale a wall."

—Verses 20-29, NIV

"The righteousness of which David boasted was not his own, for he was willing to admit that he was not free from impurity. Rather it indicates purity of motive and integrity of heart as contrasted with hypocrisy and wickedness. Our character gives its shape to our thoughts of God."[9] How we behave and how we think matters greatly. It not only affects who we are but it gives shape, too, to the quality of passion that never lets go of God no matter what happens either around us or in us—even in our sin. No matter our failures or compromises, as with David, it can always be the purpose of our heart to be true to God.[10] It is that purpose that God reads and protects in our behalf. "You, O Lord, keep my lamp burning," David exclaims. The light of his passion for God would have long gone out had it not been for God's gracious presence amidst the darkness. "He who began a good work in you will carry it on to completion until the day of Christ Jesus," Paul writes confidently (Phil. 1:6, NIV). "I know the one in whom I trust, and I am sure that he is able to guard what I have entrusted to him until the day of his return" (2 Tim. 1:12, NLT). God's mercy, God's grace, God's love, God's presence, and God's sovereign providence in his behalf all characterize David's life. His fugitive years are a gospel story. Faith on the run is about God doing for David what he could never do for himself.

That's what we need when faith is on the run. "For who is God besides the Lord?" (Ps. 18:31, NIV). "With your help, I can advance against a troop. With my God I can leap over a wall" (verse 29, paraphrase). How else can our passion for God be sustained? No wonder that God is ever worthy of it!

---

[1] Philip Yancey, *Reaching for the Invisible God,* p. 192.

[2] Gordon MacDonald, *Restoring Your Spiritual Passion,* p. 37.

[3] Ellen G. White, *This Day With God* (Washington, D.C.: Review and Herald Pub. Assn., 1979), p. 277.

[4] ————, *Our High Calling* (Washington, D.C.: Review and Herald Pub. Assn., 1961), p. 215.

[5] Oswald Chambers, *My Utmost for His Highest,* reading for February 14.

[6] Peter C. Craigie, *Psalm 1-50,* p. 173.

[7] Eugene Peterson, *Leap Over a Wall,* pp. 205, 206.

[8] F. B. Meyer, Gems *From the Psalms,* p. 29.

[9] *Ibid.*

[10] *Ibid.,* p. 690.